David Gascoyne was born in 1916 in Harrow, Middlesex, and educated at Salisbury Cathedral School and the Regent Street Polytechnic, London. His first collection of poetry, *Roman Balcony and Other Poems* was published when he was sixteen, and in 1933 Cobden-Sanderson brought out his novel *Opening Day*. Both books are remarkable achievements for an adolescent, and they were followed by the equally striking poetry collections *Man's Life Is This Meat* (1936) and *Hölderlin's Madness* (1938), which established his reputation as one of the most original voices of the 1930s.
Gascoyne was among the earliest champions of Surrealism: in 1935 his *A Short Survey of Surrealism* was published, and in the next year he was one of the organisers of the London International Surrealist Exhibition. From this period, and during his time living in France in 1937-39, date his friendships with Dalí, Max Ernst, André Breton, Paul Eluard and Pierre Jean Jouve. As well as becoming internationally celebrated as a poet – especially after publication of his *Poems 1937-1942*, with its Graham Sutherland images – Gascoyne became highly regarded as a translator, notably of Hölderlin and of the leading French Surrealists.
After the war Gascoyne again lived in France (1947-48 and 1953-64), partly in Paris and partly in Provence. He consolidated his reputation with *A Vagrant and Other Poems* (1950), and with *Night Thoughts* (1956), commissioned by Douglas Cleverdon for BBC Radio. His *Collected Poems*, published by Oxford University Press in 1965, were reprinted six times. In 1994 Enitharmon published a substantial volume of *Selected Poems*.
David Gascoyne now lives with his wife, Judy, at Northwood on the Isle of Wight. He has recently been made a Chevalier dans l'Ordre des Arts et Lettres by the French Ministry of Culture for his lifelong services to French literature.

DAVID GASCOYNE

Selected
Verse Translations

Edited by
Alan Clodd and Robin Skelton

with an introduction by
Roger Scott

ENITHARMON PRESS LONDON
1996

Published in 1996
by the Enitharmon Press
36 St George's Avenue
London N7 0HD

Distributed in Europe
by Password (Books) Ltd.
23 New Mount Street
Manchester, M4 4DE

Distributed in the USA and Canada
by Dufour Editions Inc.
PO Box 7, Chester Springs
PA 19425, USA

ISBN 1 870612 33 7 (paper)
ISBN 1 870612 38 8 (cloth edition, limited to 50 signed copies)

The front cover image is David Gascoyne's
collage *Anarchist Arabesque* (1952);
the photograph of Mr Gascoyne on the back
cover is reproduced by kind permission
of Mark Gerson.

Set in 10pt Bembo by Bryan Williamson, Frome,
and printed in Great Britain by
The Cromwell Press, Wiltshire

ACKNOWLEDGEMENTS

The Enitharmon Press gratefully acknowledges the
support and encouragement of the Translation
Advisory Group at the Arts Council of England,
the Elephant Trust and the Ministère des Affaires
Etrangères, Sous-direction de la Politique du Livre
et des Bibliothèques.

DAVID GASCOYNE: SELECT BIBLIOGRAPHY

Poetry

Roman Balcony and Other Poems (London, Lincoln Williams, 1932)

Man's Life Is This Meat (London, Parton Press, 1936)

Hölderlin's Madness (London, Dent, 1938)

Poems 1937-1942 (London, Editions: Poetry London, 1943; reprinted 1944, 1948)

A Vagrant and Other Poems (London, John Lehmann, 1950)

Night Thoughts (London, André Deutsch, and New York, Grove Press, 1956; Paris, Alyscamps Press, 1995)

Collected Poems, edited by Robin Skelton (London, Oxford University Press & André Deutsch, 1965; reprinted 1966, 1970, 1978, 1982, 1984)

Penguin Modern Poets 17, with Kathleen Raine and W.S. Graham (London, Penguin Books, 1970)

The Sun at Midnight: Poems and Aphorisms (London, Enitharmon Press, 1970)

Three Poems (London, Enitharmon Press, 1976)

Early Poems (Warwick, Greville Press, 1980)

La Mano del Poeta, bi-lingual selection of poems, edited by Francesca Romani Paci (Genoa, Edizioni S. Marco dei Giustiniani, 1982). Awarded the Premio Biella–Poesia Europea 1982

Five Early Uncollected Poems (Leamington Spa, Other Branch Readings, 1984)

Collected Poems 1988 (Oxford University Press, 1988; reprinted 1988)

Extracts from 'A Kind of Declaration' & Prelude to a New Fin-de-Siècle (Warwick, Greville Press, 1988)

Tankens Doft, selection of poems, edited by Lars–Inge Nilsson (Lund: Ellerströms, 1988)

Miserere: poèmes 1937-1942 (Paris, Granit, 1989)

Three Remanences (London, privately printed, 1994)

Selected Poems (London, Enitharmon Press, 1994)

Prose

Opening Day (novel; London, Cobden–Sanderson, 1933)

A Short Survey of Surrealism (London, Cobden–Sanderson, 1935; London, Frank Cass & Co., 1970; San Francisco, City Lights Books, 1982)

Thomas Carlyle (London, Longman, Green & Co., 1952; reprinted 1963, 1969)

Paris Journal 1937-1939, with a preface by Lawrence Durrell
   (London, Enitharmon Press, 1978)
Journal, 1936-37 (London, Enitharmon Press, 1980)
Journal de Paris et d'ailleurs, 1936-1942, translated by Christine Jordis
   (Paris, Flammarion, 1984)
Rencontres avec Benjamin Fondane (Cognac, Arcane 17, 1984)
Collected Journals, 1937-42, introduced by Kathleen Raine (London,
   Skoob Books Publishing, 1990)
Lawrence Durrell (London, privately printed, 1993)
The Fire of Vision: David Gascoyne and George Barker, edited and
   introduced by Roger Scott (London, privately printed, 1996)
Selected Essays, edited by Alan Clodd, Roger Scott and
   Stephen Stuart-Smith (London, Enitharmon Press, 1997)

Translations
Salvador Dalí, *Conquest of the Irrational* (New York, Julien Levy,
   1935)
Benjamin Péret, *A Bunch of Carrots: Twenty Poems* (London, Roger
   Roughton, 1936; trans. with Humphrey Jennings; second
   edition published as *Remove Your Hat*, 1936)
André Breton, *What is Surrealism?* (London, Faber, 1936)
Paul Eluard, *Thorns of Thunder*, Selected Poems edited by George
   Reavey (London, Europa Press & Stanley Nott, 1936;
   trans. with Samuel Beckett, Denis Devlin, Eugène Jolas,
   Man Ray, George Reavey and Ruthven Todd)
Collected Verse Translations, edited by Alan Clodd and Robin Skelton
   (London, Oxford University Press, 1970)
André Breton and Philippe Soupault, *The Magnetic Fields* (London,
   Atlas Press, 1985)
Benjamin Péret, *Remove Your Hat and Other Works* (London, Atlas
   Press, 1985; trans. with Martin Sorrell)
Pierre Jean Jouve, *The Unconscious, Spirituality, Catastrophe* (Child
   Okeford, Words Press, 1988)
Three Translations (Child Okeford, Words Press, 1988)
Poems of Milosz (London, Enitharmon Press, 1993)
Pierre Jean Jouve, *The Present Greatness of Mozart* (Birmingham,
   Delos Press, 1996)
Selected Verse Translations, edited by Alan Clodd and Robin Skelton,
   with an introduction by Roger Scott (London, Enitharmon
   Press, 1996)

CONTENTS

x

PREFACE*

David Gascoyne's first translations of French poetry appeared in 1936 when he was twenty years old, and his contributions to Roger Roughton's *Contemporary Poetry and Prose* and especially to the surrealist issue of that magazine were responsible for introducing much surrealist poetry to English readers for the first time. He regarded himself as a surrealist poet at this period, but after the publication of the second collection of his own poetry, *Man's Life Is This Meat* (1936), and his *Short Survey of Surrealism* in the same year he ceased following the orthodox surrealist line. Nevertheless, in his translation of Benjamin Péret's *Remove Your Hat* (1936) and in his contributions to periodicals Gascoyne continued to make surrealist poetry available to English readers. His interest was, however, now far more in the visionary than in the Freudian implications of the movement and this found an outlet in *Hölderlin's Madness* (1938), a series of translations of Hölderlin interspersed with poems of his own that formed an artistic and philosophical unity. From this time onwards he translated fewer surrealist poems and concentrated more upon mystical and philosophical verse, especially that of Paul Eluard, Pierre Jean Jouve, and Jules Supervielle. The present volume does not pretend to being a complete collection of all his translations; some selection has been necessary. It is, however, we believe, a satisfactorily full and balanced compilation. We have used the phrase 'Verse Translations' in our title to indicate our exclusion of essays, but we have allowed ourselves to include some prose poems. We have also included the whole of *Hölderlin's Madness*, regarding this work as a unity which would be marred by selection, and feeling that the translations cannot properly be appreciated out of context, though Gascoyne's original poems may be.

Many of these translations have appeared in David Gascoyne's books. An almost equally large number, however, have only appeared in periodicals, and some are printed here for the first time.

In editing this book we have greatly benefited from the advice of Kathleen Raine and the researches of Arthur Uphill. We are also grateful to Mrs Jenny Stratford and the staff of the Depart-

---

* This was written by Robin Skelton as the preface to David Gascoyne's *Collected Verse Translations* (1970).

ment of Manuscripts at the British Museum for assistance in the study of the Gascoyne manuscripts in the Museum's possession.

ROBIN SKELTON
The University of Victoria
British Columbia

NOTE TO THE 1996 EDITION

This new edition of David Gascoyne's translations has been augmented by the inclusion of many of the considerable number of translations, mostly from contemporary French poets, which he has made since the publication in 1970 by the Oxford University Press of his *Collected Verse Translations*. A small number of translations which appeared in that volume have been omitted from this new selection.

I have been fortunate in being able to include hitherto unpublished early translations of poems by Friedrich Hölderlin, Pierre Jean Jouve and Stéphane Mallarmé which have been discovered in the Gascoyne notebooks in the British Library and elsewhere.

I am grateful to David and Judy Gascoyne for their hospitality and to David for his patience in answering my many questions; to Roger Scott for his enthusiasm and for his tirelessness in searching for and locating so many translations in little-known small magazines and periodicals; to Mrs Sally Brown and the staff at the Manuscripts Department of the British Library for their helpfulness and courtesy.

My publisher Stephen Stuart-Smith has been very supportive and patient and Colin Benford's *David Gascoyne: A Bibliography of his Works (1929 – 1985)* has been invaluable; Jeremy Reed has been consistent in his interest and encouragement.

ALAN CLODD
February 1996

INTRODUCTION

The poet David Gascoyne is still translating, sixty years after Julien Levy first published his *Conquest of the Irrational* from the French of Salvador Dalí.[1] For too long, and unaccountably, Gascoyne's *Collected Verse Translations* of 1970[2] have been out of print, so that at least one whole generation has remained largely unaware of his earlier, and remarkable, work in this field. The publication of this new volume of *Selected Verse Translations* presents to old and new readers his translations of European (and other) poets, dating from the 1930s to the present decade.

★   ★   ★

From 1930 to 1932, while a pupil at Regent Street Polytechnic Secondary School, Gascoyne regularly walked home down Charing Cross Road to visit Zwemmer's Bookshop and to buy back numbers of *transition* (sic) and *La Révolution Surréaliste* (1924–9). He told Michèle Duclos in an interview conducted in June 1984 that he also purchased the surrealist number of *This Quarter* and began to collect *Le Surréalisme au service de la Révolution* and later, *Minotaure*, after he had met the surrealists in Paris.[3] 'I first began,' writes Gascoyne, 'to read Baudelaire, Rimbaud and Mallarmé in my teens, and then went on to read most contemporary French poets, the surrealists in particular'.[4]

By the mid-1930s, Gascoyne's record as published poet, novelist, essayist, art critic and reviewer could be considered nothing short of prodigious. By the end of that 'grim' decade, during which he made

---

[1] New York, 1935. *La conquête de l'irrationel* was translated at Dalí's request. After spending more than a week with the Spaniard and Gala, his wife, at their Paris studio, dominated by the painting *The Great Masturbator* (later renamed *A Portrait of the Marquis de Sade* in honour of André Breton), Gascoyne's reward for translating the essay was 'a handsome example of Dalí's draughtsmanship, as well as the cost of the fare I needed to return to England'. (Typescript of Gascoyne's review of Tim McGirk, *Wicked Lady: Salvador Dalí's Muse* (Hutchinson, 1986).

[2] Edited by Robin Skelton and Alan Clodd (Oxford University Press).

[3] 'Entretiens avec David Gascoyne (Londres)' in *Cahiers sur la Poésie* 2 (1984), 'Numéro special David Gascoyne', pp. 18–19. See also Gascoyne's 'Introductory Notes' to his *Collected Poems 1988* (Oxford University Press), p. xiv, and to *Selected Poems* (Enitharmon, 1994), p. xii.

[4] From the typescript, 'Poetry in Britain Today' (n.d.). See also Lucien Jenkins, 'David Gascoyne in Interview', in *Stand*, Vol. 33, No. 2 (Spring 1992), p. 24.

a number of long visits to Paris, and lived in France,[5] he was celebrated, too, for his translations of French poetry which had appeared in book form or as single contributions to such periodicals of the time as *New Verse, Contemporary Poetry and Prose*, the Paris based *Delta* (formerly *The Booster*), *Babel* and *The New Statesman and Nation*.[6]

In 1933 Geoffrey Grigson included in number six of *New Verse* Gascoyne's translations of poems by Giacometti and Ribemont-Dessaignes. The previous edition had contained 'And the Seventh Dream is the Dream of Isis', 'the result of my first attempt to produce a sequence of poetry according to the orthodox surrealist formula'.[7] Gascoyne's essay 'French Poetry of Today' appeared in *Everyman* in August 1934 after his return in December of the previous year from his first, three-month visit to France which, financed largely by the advance royalties he had received for the publication of his only novel, *Opening Day*, was 'a momentous first encounter', as he wrote in a letter three years later to Benjamin Fondane. 'For me it was a heady adolescent ferment of ideas, ambitions, poetry, sexual experiences, all of which now seem to me quite unreal.'[8] He had brought back with him a gouache by Max Ernst, as well as copies of recent collections by André Breton and Paul Eluard (including *L'immaculée conception*), Tristan Tzara and Benjamin Péret, though he had not yet then made initial personal contact with any of the representative writers of the surrealist group.

Back in Paris in 1935, Gascoyne was researching the book on the surrealist movement his publishers, Cobden-Sanderson, had commissioned him to write. He was already in correspondence with Eluard, and his friend S. W. Hayter took him in the summer of that year to meet Breton who made a great impression on him. Although he visited Paul and Nusch Eluard, and saw René Crevel two weeks before he committed suicide, Gascoyne was unable then to meet

[5] Between 1937 and 1939, as he would do much later, 1953-64, largely in Aix-en-Provence.

[6] *Cahiers du Sud*, No. 220 (Janvier 1940), published his 'Strophes Elégiaques à la mémoire d'Alban Berg', translated from the elegy he had first written in English but judged to be unsatisfactory.

[7] 'Introductory Notes' to *Collected Poems 1988* and *Selected Poems* (1994), pp. xiv and xii.

[8] 'Meetings with Benjamin Fondane', in *Aquarius* 17/18 (London: 1986-7), p. 24. The letter is dated 24.7.37. 'Surrealism really seemed to be the bomb which could break open to me this dull mediocre world.'

Tzara, Philippe Soupault or Robert Desnos because of certain exclusions or expulsions from the surrealist group. His ground-breaking *A Short Survey of Surrealism*, the first full-length account of the movement in English, was published in November; the main text was followed by Gascoyne's translations of poems by Breton, Dalí, Eluard, Hugnet and Tzara (and by Ruthven Todd of poems by René Char and Péret).

In June 1936, his close friend Roger Roughton published two poems by Gascoyne in the second, 'Surrealist', number of his periodical *Contemporary Poetry and Prose*, together with nine translations from the French of Char, Buñuel, Eluard, Breton, Prassinos, Rosey, Péret and Henry. Translations from Dalí and Péret appeared in the next number.[9] In the previous month, two translations from poems by Arp and Eluard had been included in *New Verse*, No. 21.

This was to be a year of several major publications for the twenty-year-old poet. *Man's Life Is This Meat*[10] was issued by David Archer at his Parton Press in May, followed in June by *A Bunch of Carrots*, the first (and censored) selected translations by Gascoyne and Humphrey Jennings of Péret, published by Roughton. The revised edition, with its less provocative title, *Remove Your Hat*, came out later that month,[11] as did Gascoyne's translation of Breton's *What is surrealism?*, published by Faber and Faber (in their Criterion Miscellany No. 43). In July, Gascoyne was one of several co-translators[12] represented in *Paul Eluard – Thorns of Thunder* (edited by George Reavey). 'No English poet was more thorough and intimate in his knowledge of that movement [surrealism]; no Englishman a better translator of the French surrealists,' writes Glyn Pursglove in his entry on Gascoyne in *Contemporary Poets*, 5th edition (Chicago and London, St James Press, 1991, p. 331).

Although he made frequent long visits to France during the next three years, this was not to be a period of intense literary activity. What is very apparent from entries in his Journal for 1937 is a growing disenchantment with the surrealist group. However, Gascoyne

9   August/September. Gascoyne's translation 'From the Deserts of Love' by Rimbaud was in *Contemporary Poetry and Prose*, No. 9 (Spring 1937).

10   'With the exception of Nos. 1-6 the poems in this collection are surrealist poems'.

11   See Gascoyne's introduction to *Remove Your Hat and other works* by Benjamin Péret, published by Atlas Press in 1985.

12   The others were George Reavey, Samuel Beckett, Denis Devlin, Eugène Jolas, Man Ray, Ruthven Todd. The collection was published by Reavey's Europa Press with Stanley Nott.

was about to make one of the most crucial literary and personal contacts of his life, deriving initially from his regular visits to the British Library Reading Room at the end of 1935 and the beginning of 1936 when, contemplating a sequel to his *A Short Survey of Surrealism*, he was researching for a study of Rimbaud[13] and was supplied with Benjamin Fondane's *Rimbaud le voyou*. This meeting with Fondane 'at a critical moment in my youth was both providential and decisive'. However, the meeting was even more significant than that. In Fondane, he 'found someone who explained to me why surrealism no longer satisfied me as a means of poetic expression, nor as a means of revolutionising human subjectivity'.[14] He corresponded with the French writer and eventually they met towards the end of the summer of 1937 in a little town, La Varenne Saint-Hilaire, south of Paris. This was followed by a series of meetings there during the autumn and winter of the following year.

In the late autumn of 1937 Gascoyne was to make another vital discovery, a copy of Pierre Jean Jouve's translations, *Poèmes de la Folie de Hölderlin*, which 'marked a turning-point in my approach to poetry'.[15] The shock-waves, as with Fondane, would continue to reverberate in his daily life and his development as a writer. In September 1937 Gascoyne began to produce versions of poems by Friedrich Hölderlin. J. M. Dent published his *Hölderlin's Madness* in 1938. An introductory note, following an essay on Hölderlin, acknowledges his indebtedness to Jouve's French translation and states: 'The poems which follow are not a translation of selected poems by Hölderlin, but a free adaptation, introduced and linked together by entirely original poems ['Figures in a Landscape', 'Orpheus in the Underworld', 'Tenebrae', 'Epilogue']. The whole constitutes what may perhaps be regarded as a persona.'

Francis Scarfe reviewed the collection in Julian Symons's *Twentieth Century Verse*, No. 11 (July 1938): 'In revealing us Hölderlin, Mr Gascoyne has done his generation a service. . . . He translates imaginatively, and the four poems of his own in this book show that he is

---

[13]   To be called 'Diabolic Angel', but never completed.

[14]   *Aquarius* 17/18, op. cit., p. 23. By the time the catalogue was issued for the Exhibition of Surrealist Objects at the London Gallery in the winter of 1937, containing three pieces by Gascoyne (later to be re-titled 'Three Verbal Objects', and dedicated to Humphrey Jennings), he had, in his own words, 'virtually ceased writing in the surrealist vein'. Gascoyne wrote the preface to *Benjamin Fondane: Le Mal des Fantômes*, Collected Poems (Editions Plasma, 1980), pp. 7-14.

[15]   'Introductory Notes' to *CP 1988* and to *Selected Poems* (1994), pp. xvii and xiv.

worthy of the poet he admires' (p. 76). In an essay on Gascoyne nine years later, Derek Stanford makes the point that the impact of the German poet is modified by two translations (given the use Gascoyne made of Jouve's *Poèmes de la Folie de Hölderlin*), 'a feature which would lead us to expect a certain anaemic quality in the work. Nothing however, is further from the truth: power of image, clarity of language, and simplicity of music characterize the verse.... This small book of forty-eight pages,' continues Stanford, 'is undoubtedly one of the finest works of poetic "naturalization" which we have seen in the last twenty years.'[16]

In his *Collected Journals 1936-42*, Gascoyne writes of Jouve: 'I know of no one who has so fully expressed the *apocalyptic* atmosphere of our time or with so strong an accent of the "sublime".' (January 1939, p. 243) He was to write in 'My Indebtedness to Jouve' in the literary review *Adam* 422/24 in 1980[17] that he was proud to have been the translator of the introductory essay to Jouve's study, *Grandeur actuelle de Mozart*, published by Cyril Connolly in *Horizon* in 1940.[18] Tambimuttu published Gascoyne's translation of Jouve's 'The Unconscious, Spirituality, Catastrophe' in *Poetry* (London) in 1941,[19] a translation of Jouve's poem 'The Most Beautiful, Most Naked and Most Tragic Splendour' (later retitled 'Nada') had already appeared in *Delta* (No. 1, Easter 1939), and others would follow in wartime in *Poetry* (London), *Kingdom Come*, and *New Directions*.

Poems 1937-1942 was published Editions Poetry London (Nicolson & Watson) in 1943, with eight striking reproductions in colour (including those for the front and back covers) of designs by Graham Sutherland. This new collection, his third, comprised fifty-seven poems, together with five translations of poems by Jouve, a rendering of a piece by Jules Supervielle, and the revised version, in French, of his elegy for the composer Alban Berg. Stephen Spender welcomed the publication of *Poems 1937-1942* in his 'Lessons of Poetry 1943' in

---

[16] Stanford, *The Freedom of Poetry: Studies in Contemporary Verse* (Falcon Press, 1947), pp. 46, 47.

[17] This short essay was accompanied by translations of four poems by Jouve: 'Tempo Di Mozart', 'Viaticum', 'In the Common Grave' and 'Don Juan'.

[18] Vol. 1, No. 2, pp. 84–94. This translation is to be reissued in 1996 by Peter Baldwin's Delos Press.

[19] No. 4 (January/February), pp. 112-14. The original formed the 'Avant-Propos' to Jouve's collection *Sueur de Sang*. This translation was reissued in a limited edition in 1988 by Words Press.

Horizon, No. 51 (March 1944): '[it] may count as the most important event in poetry in 1943' (pp. 211-12). Earlier, in his long essay, Spender had written:

> For a poet, translating foreign poetry is the best possible exercise in interpretation. A poet's aim as a translator (from this viewpoint) should not be absolute accuracy, but to return to the source of the poet's inspiration and to create a parallel poem in the English language. Thus the poet gains sympathy with poetic experiences outside his own, and with techniques outside the ones he would use to express his own experience. Poets in the past have devoted enormous powers to the unrewarding task of translating. Today, there seems a regrettable tendency to treat translators as a race apart. Yet a translator is no good unless he happens to be a poet.... So poets can go to school and do exercises. All the great poets of the past and present have done so, with few exceptions, though the schooling of the moderns has been less direct and obvious in method, since modern poetry has no technical aims binding all poets to a common discipline. In a serious poet whose work has appeared this year, David Gascoyne, we see the Exercise in his poems written in French. (pp. 208-9)

Many years later, Philip Gardner was to observe with some acuity that the language Gascoyne uses in his translations of Jouve 'has sometimes a marked resemblance to his own densely packed lines in *Poems 1937-1942*. Certainly Gascoyne's mastery of the alexandrine – a difficult line-length to manage in English – derives from his knowledge of French poetry.'[20] This accords with Yves Bonnefoy's view, expressed in his essay 'Translating Poetry', that while 'the translator need [not] be...a poet...It definitely implies that if he himself is a writer he will be unable to keep his translating separate from his own work.'[21] There were three translations from the French of Jules Supervielle in Gascoyne's next collection, *A Vagrant and other poems*, published by John Lehmann in 1950.

★   ★   ★

---

[20]   See his entry on Gascoyne in *Dictionary of Literary Biography*, edited by Donald Stanford, Vol. 20, *British Poets 1914-1945* (Detroit, Michigan, Gale Research Co., 1983), p. 144.

[21]   *P.N. Review*, No. 45 (1985), p. 6, translated by John Alexander and Clive Wilmer.

Numerous translations by Gascoyne from the work of the older surrealists and of contemporary French poets, together with versions of Leopardi, Georg Trakl and Xie Chuang, have been published since the *Collected Verse Translations* of 1970. They appeared in periodicals, diverse little magazines and anthologies, during a particularly fertile period between 1979 and 1988, following his marriage to Judy Lewis in 1975. It was a time when he wrote little poetry of his own. *Poems of Milosz* came out in 1993,[22] preceded in 1985 (Atlas Press) by his translation of *The Magnetic Fields* by Breton and Soupault, the first 'automatic text' (published in its complete form in 1920). Brian Merrikin-Hill's assertion that 'no one other than Gascoyne could have translated this book with a mastery of English and French and the necessary sympathetic fluidity of mind'[23] seems incontrovertible. Michèle Duclos had asked Gascoyne in 1984 what seemed to him essential when translating a poem. He replied that 'one always tries to achieve a balance. ... The translation that I have made of *Les Champs Magnétiques* is a little special because one must retain the essence of the literal sense while being fully aware that it is a transcription of the unconscious and of associations of images.'

In the same interview, Duclos asked him 'Why do you translate? Does that particularly interest you?' 'Oh, yes!' was the response, 'it always has done. And at times when one can't write poems oneself, it represents a way of creating equivalents of poems that one likes or admires. Rarely have I translated a poem that I haven't liked.' (In his essay 'Translating Poetry', Yves Bonnefoy makes the observation, 'If a work does not compel us, it is untranslatable'.) Gascoyne continued, 'Above all, I like to translate poems by poets whom I know personally, because it seems easier to put myself into their frame of mind with that background knowledge'.[24]

Some years ago, in a conversation with Kathleen Raine, the surrealist poet Philippe Soupault, acknowledging Gascoyne's extraordinary sympathy with France and French poetry, described him as 'a French poet writing in English'. Certainly Gascoyne's is a unique voice in modern English poetry. Donald Hall contends that Gascoyne

---

[22]   O. V. de L. Milosz (Enitharmon Poetry Pamphlets).

[23]   Review, 'The Transparent Mirror' in *Temenos* 7 (1986), p. 276. The reviewer in *Time Out* chose to refer particularly to the introduction by Gascoyne: '[it] is as intelligent and passionate as his translation.'

[24]   Op. cit., p. 30, my translation.

'remains the English author who has most absorbed the experiments of the modern movement in France'.[25]

On 18 May 1981 the British Council and the Centre Georges Pompidou jointly celebrated Gascoyne's European reputation in 'Homage to David Gascoyne', a soirée of readings of his poetry in French and English. In 1984 Flammarion published Gascoyne's journals in French, *Journal de Paris et d'ailleurs 1936-1942*, in a translation by Christine Jordis, some eight years before they appeared in their complete form in English, with the addition of the Wartime Journal 1940-42. His work is now being read and studied in French universities,[26] as it is by academics and poetry-lovers throughout the world. And in this, his eightieth year, David Gascoyne is to be presented by the French Minister of Culture with the prestigious award of Chevalier dans l'Ordre des Arts et Lettres, in recognition of his services to literature and art in France.

The Guardian critic, Redmond O'Hanlon, reviewing the première in Dublin of the Irish poet Derek Mahon's version of Racine's *Phèdre* early in 1996, expressed the view that 'Translation is a complex negotiation between different cultures and rhetorics'.[27] As far as I know David Gascoyne has not translated Racine, but no other poet in English over the past sixty years has done more for French poetry.

ROGER SCOTT
University of Northumbria
March 1996

---

[25] In Stephen Spender and Donald Hall (eds): entry on Gascoyne in their *Concise Encyclopaedia of English & American Poets and Poetry* (Hutchinson, 1970).

[26] A selection of Gascoyne's poems translated into French under the title *Miserere* was published by Granit (Paris) in their 'Collection du Miroir' in 1989.

[27] 16 February 1996, p. 2.

Guillaume Apollinaire (1880 – 1918)

FRANCIS PICABIA

Praxiteles is a bandage-maker
Your right big toe
Has hurled abuse
At the horseman who in Venice has three
In Asia Minor or in maybe Champagne
Where the stags bring their antlers
For you know which gentlemen
And if you dance the tango
Noli me tangere

From *Le Guetteur mélancolique*

André Breton (1896 – 1966)

THE SPECTRAL ATTITUDES

I attach no importance to life
I pin not the least of life's butterflies to importance
I do not matter to life
But the branches of salt the white branches
All the shadow bubbles
And the sea-anemones
Come down and breathe within my thoughts
They come from tears that are not mine
From steps I do not take that are steps twice
And of which the sand remembers the flood-tide
The bars are in the cage
And the birds come down from far above to sing before these bars
A subterranean passage unites all perfumes
A woman pledged herself there one day
This woman became so bright that I could no longer see her
With these eyes which have seen my own self burning
I was then already as old as I am now
And I watched over myself and my thoughts like a nightwatchman
    in an immense factory
Keeping watch alone
The circus always enchants the same tramlines
The plaster figures have lost nothing of their expression
They who bit the smile's fig
I know of a drapery in a forgotten town
If it pleased me to appear to you wrapped in this drapery
You would think that your end was approaching
Like mine
At last the fountains would understand that you must not say
    Fountain
The wolves are clothed in mirrors of snow
I have a boat detached from all climates
I am dragged along by an ice-pack with teeth of flame
I cut and cleave the wood of this tree that will always be green
A musician is caught up in the strings of his instrument
The skull and crossbones of the time of any childhood story
Goes on board a ship that is as yet its own ghost only

Perhaps there is a hilt to this sword
But already there is a duel in this hilt
During the duel the combatants are unarmed
Death is the least offence
The future never comes

The curtains that have never been raised
Float to the windows of houses that are to be built
The beds made of lilies
Slide beneath the lamps of dew
There will come an evening
The nuggets of light become still underneath the blue moss
The hands that tie and untie the knots of love and of air
Keep all their transparency for those who have eyes to see
They see the palms of hands
The crowns in eyes
But the brazier of crowns and palms
Can scarcely be lit in the deepest part of the forest
There where the stags bend their heads to examine the years
Nothing more than a feeble beating is heard
From which sound a thousand louder or softer sounds proceed
And the beating goes on and on
There are dresses that vibrate
And their vibration is in unison with the beating
When I wish to see the faces of those that wear them
A great fog rises from the ground
At the bottom of the steeples behind the most elegant reservoirs of
    life and wealth
In the gorges which hide themselves between two mountains
On the sea at the hour when the sun cools down
Those who make signs to me are separated by stars
And yet the carriage overturned at full speed
Carries as far as my last hesitation
That awaits me down there in the town where the statues of bronze
    and of stone have changed places with statues of wax
Banyans banyans.

/ André Breton

POSTMAN CHEVAL

We are the birds always charmed by you from the top of these
    belvederes
And that each night form a blossoming branch between your shoulders
    and the arms of your well beloved wheelbarrow
Which we tear out swifter than sparks at your wrist
We are the sighs of the glass statue that raises itself on its elbow when
    man sleeps
And shining holes appear in his bed
Holes through which stags with coral antlers can be seen in a glade
And naked women at the bottom of a mine
You remembered then you got up you got out of the train
Without glancing at the locomotive attacked by immense barometric
    roots
Complaining about its murdered boilers in the virgin forest
Its funnels smoking jacinths and moulting blue snakes
Then we went on, plants subject to metamorphosis
Each night making signs that man may understand
While his house collapses and he stands amazed before the singular
    packing-cases
Sought after by his bed with the corridor and the staircase
The staircase goes on without end
It leads to a millstone door it enlarges suddenly in a public square
It is made of the backs of swans with a spreading wing for banisters
it turns inside out as though it were going to bite itself
But no, it is content at the sound of our feet to open all its steps like
    drawers
Drawers of bread drawers of wine drawers of soap drawers of ice
    drawers of stairs
Drawers of flesh with handsfull of hair
Without turning round you seized the trowel with which breasts are
    made
We smiled at you you held us round the waist
And we took the positions of your pleasure
Motionless under our lids for ever as a woman delights to see man
After having made love.

CARDS ON THE DUNES

To Giuseppe Ungaretti

The timetable of hollow flowers and of prominent cheekbones invites us to quit the volcanic equine eye-pits for the birds' bath-tubs. On a red checked napkin are laid out the days of the year. The air is no longer so pure, the road no longer so broad as the celebrated clarion-call. The perishable evenings which are the knees' place on a praying-stool get carried away in a suitcase painted with great mites. Little ribbed bicycles ride round the counter. The ears of fish, more forked than honeysuckle, listen to the blue oils come down. Among the dazzling burnouses whose load's lost in the curtains, I recognize a man of my own blood.

From *Clair de Terre* (1923)

THE HERMIT-CRAB SAYS:

I'VE KNOWN A LOT

General Eblé remoteness
Curl-papers
The incompatibilities of mood according to astronomy
A personification of Good-morning
The sad intoxication of wine-tasters
At present I hover over the falling of leaves and I sleep with my head
     in the feathers like a saucepan
It's all the same to me since the singular signals with which the dust
     made its jealousy plain

/ *André Breton*

CURTAINS

Mousetraps of the soul after turning off the white radiator siesta of
    the sacraments
Connecting-rod of the boat
Raft
Pretty stranded seaweeds they come in all colours
Shivers on returning home at night
Two heads like the plates of a pair of scales

NEVER HAD A START

Tiles oil isle bill-hook
The president defends himself clumsily with an axe
It's going to be necessary to take cover
The best workmen are to be feared
One can no longer see more than two feet ahead
The firewood woman
I don't understand this meeting on leaving the law-courts
Belt of medals
Sawdust in a circle's arc on the café terraces
Cloud of grasshoppers sediment
There are whole countries built on carcasses of fishbone
Everything is ruby-coloured seven times

GRAND LUXE

Straw-wrapped trees of high-class hotels
Prisoners pardoned for their good conduct
Solid liquid gaseous condition
Striking achievement of the sun
Steam-driven crank of the fields in the morning
Account must be kept of the admirable distance
I am the one to take the first steps
If only my friends hadn't been turned into statues of salt
Space of a minute that I cross on horseback
Nearby sojourns in the country
Portals in the desert O these cathedrals that are pyramids of monkeys

I believe I'm mixing up civilisations odour of purple
One more news-item
My God so we shall never be
Consecration of the devil-fish on the rock-crystal
It's the brooch of Her corsage
Silver paper not paper sliver
Just as there's note-book and papyrus
Ardent ideology
Handsome calf
Trumpet of the square

RESCUE

Ability to procure
Free information
Mend your ways on earth
Happy to oblige
Here are the pleasing pickaxes of the inoffensive turning-back
The well-deserved gold
Mushroom grown in the night tomorrow it will no longer be fresh
Animating season of our desires
Opening of doors before the horsewoman

STORM IN A GLASS OF WATER

Fish-merchant friend of serious proceedings follow me carefully
I have more than one trick in my bag
With custom-made green transparencies
People have no notion of these calorimeters
Which lend their scope to our desires
Wherein seemly sentimentalities are maintained at 32°
I'm afraid of seasickness
The tutor's insufferable oar
Experiment of our lives measured according to the number of heart-
    beats
It's a very long streamlet thanks to the connivance of the nosegays
    enlivened by music

/ André Breton

BYPASS THROUGH THE SKY

Child weaves a despair of pearls
Draws inspiration from the boxes he's received for his communion
Instigates the problem of birth in the form of a neat equation in the
    key of C
Barricades his window with his eyelashes
Plays with his little sister's prayer which is more silvery than his own
Endures the ill-treatments
Of two to three
Multiplies himself in the manner of his book's microbes notably by
    schizo-genesis the one which separates itself from him has wings
He thinks about the beautiful karyokinesis
During mass

THE YOUNG SPROUTS

The theatre footlights and the practice-bar
Form of nasturtiums
The stage is sand-strewn with little multicoloured spaces for the
    national anthems
Joke over
From concession to concession
The neat fingerprints on the calendar
King of the sentimental meadows in which top-hats are willows
Therefore a nigger king

LAND OF COLOUR

Worms follow the canals of the mounds and meet barges of crystal
    drawn by moles
They fear the sun's glare and the spade's shaft both equally blue
Mutually rob each other of hope
The dews set out goblets on all sides
The earwigs drink
They listen at doors and dwell in tool-boxes
Tin-tacks
Clove-pinks

Jerome's Cock Contest
A breaking of bans followed by hand-bills
Black sand
Moulding of paradise
Solar inspection then genuine freshness
I dream of summer in the dormitory
Someone says to me What have you got instead of a heart

From *Les Champs Magnétiques* (1920)

/ André Breton

André Breton (1896 – 1966)
and Paul Eluard (1895 – 1952)

FORCE OF HABIT

The table is placed in the dining-room; the taps give out clear water, soft water, tepid water, scented water. The bed is as large for two as for one. After the bud will come the leaf and after the leaf the flower and after rain fine weather. Because it is time, the eyes open, the body stands up, the hand stretches out, the fire is lit, the smile contends with night's wrinkles for their unmalicious curve. And they are the clock's hands that open, that stand up, that stretch out, that set light to themselves and mark the hour of the smile. The sun's ray goes about the house in a white blouse. It's going to snow again, a few drops of blood are going to fall again at about five o'clock, but that'll be nothing. Oh! I was frightened, I suddenly thought there was no longer any street outside the window, but it is there just the same as ever. The chemist is even raising his metal shutters. There will soon be more people at the wheel than at the mill. Work is sharpened, hammered, thinned down, reckoned out. Once more the hand takes pleasure in finding the security of sleep in the familiar implement.

Provided that it lasts!

The mirror is a marvellous witness, changing all the time. It gives evidence calmly and with power, but when it has finished speaking you can see that it has been caught out again over everything. It is the current personification of verity.

On the hairpin-bend road obstinately tied to the legs of him who assesses today as he will assess tomorrow, on the light bearings of carelessness, a thousand steps each day espouse the steps of the vigil. They have come already and they will come again without being invited. Each one has passed that way, going from his joy to his sorrow. It is a little refuge with an enormous gas-jet. You put one foot in front of the other and then you are gone.

The walls cover themselves with pictures, the holidays sift themselves with bouquets, the mirror covers itself with vapour. As many light-houses on a stream and the stream is in the vessel of the river. Two eyes the same, for the use of your single face – two eyes covered with the same ants. Green is almost uniformly spread over the plants, the wind follows the birds, no one risks seeing the stones die.

The result is not a broken-in animal but an animal trainer. Bah! It is the indefeasible order of a ceremony already, on the whole, so very gorgeous! It is the repeating pistol which makes flowers appear in vases and smoke in the mouth.

Love, in the end, is well satisfied with seeing night clearly.

When you are no longer there, your perfume is there to search for me. I only come to get back the oracle of your weakness. My hand in your hand is so little like your hand in mine. Unhappiness, you see, unhappiness itself profits from being known. I let you share my lot, you cannot not be there, you are the proof that I exist. And everything conforms with that life which I have made to assure myself of you.

What are you thinking about?

Nothing.

From *L'Immaculée Conception* (1930)

Blaise Cendrars (1887 – 1961)

MEE TOO BUGGI

As was common among the ancient Greeks, it is
Supposed that every well–educated man should
                know how to strum the lyre
Give me the fango–fango
Let me put it up my nose
A soft and serious note comes out
of the right nostril
There is the description of landscapes
The recital of past events
An account of distant countries
Bolotoo
Papalangi
The poet among other things can describe animals
The houses are knocked over by enormous birds
The women wear too many clothes
Rhymes and rhythms all out of gear
If you make allowance for a slight amount of exaggeration
The man who amputated his leg all by himself
Made a great hit of the simple and lighthearted kind
Mee low fella
Mariwaggi beats a drum on the front doorstep of his house.

From *Dix-neuf Poèmes Élastiques* (July 1914)

René Char *(1907 – 88)*

THE RAVING MESSENGERS OF FRANTIC POETRY

The lazy suns that feed on meningitis
Go down the rivers of the middle ages
Sleep in the crevices of rocks
On a bed of papers and excrescences
They do not turn aside from the zone of rotten pincers
Like the air–balloons of hell.

GEORGES BRAQUE INTRA MUROS

In a palace surmounted by the tiara I have seen a man enter and look round at the walls. He wandered through the doleful solitude and turned towards the window. The nearby waters of the river must have eddied at the same moment, then the beauty which proceeds from a couple to a stone, then the dust of rebels in their papal sepulchre.

The four major walls began to support his hopes, the world which he had broken open and revealed, life assenting to the secret, and that heart which bursts out into colours, a heart everyone adopts as his own for better or worse.

I have seen, this Winter, that same man smile at his very low house, trimming a reed in order to draw flowers with it, I have seen him breaking through the frozen grass with a stick, be the eye which breathes and kindles the trace.

Palais des Papes, Avignon

NARROW ALTAR

A tread's heard to recede, two dogs begin to bark
And the night hides itself in a nook.
The steward in charge of shady twists
Sets off to measure the grounding for life's boat
Between the tide-mark and the harbour-mouth.
It can't delay. One can but wait.
Even with screwed-up lips he'll come to make us one,
Now that our breasts rejoin each other's so;
So much more does the race enrich the risk
Now that our castle of tar is ablaze.

Captivity golden here, and in space black.
Detest, attempt to flee, O candour of the night!
All the assets a night brings without the least unlikelihood.

From *Fenêtres dormantes et porte sur le toit* (1979)

After the Chinese of Xie Chuang (421 – 466 AD)

THE DARKENING GARDEN

The sky at sundown clarifies evening's aether,
Sprightly colour-stained clouds subside into nightfall's shade;
A light flurry of wind enlivens the dusk's murky veil,
While such light as remains illumines the wood's bluish-green.
Once the glow has been gleaned, the casement is slowly obscured.
The whole forlorn garden's now lying submerged in deep gloom.
The jade pool is shaken by surf-wraiths like white silken plumes.
The feelings of autumn echo the season's chill peals.
Should someone partake of another's amorous disposition,
Both may at last coalesce like wine-strains in a harmonious still.

René Daumal (1908 – 44)

THE POET'S LAST WORDS

From a fruit left rotting on the ground, a new tree can still arise. From this tree, new fruit by the hundredfold.

But if the poem is a fruit, the poet is not a tree. He asks you to take his words and devour them at once. For he cannot produce his fruit all by himself. Two are needed to make a poem. He who speaks is the father, whoever listens is the mother, the poem is their child. The poem that is not heard is a lost seed. Or to put it another way: the one who speaks is the mother, the poem is the egg, and whoever listens impregnates the egg. The poem that is not heard becomes a rotten egg.

★

That was what haunted the thoughts of a poet in prison under sentence of death. This was in a small country that had just been invaded by a conqueror's armies. The poet had been arrested because in a poem that he'd been singing on the roads he'd compared the sadness that was gnawing his body's flesh away to the bone to the deadly fumes of the fires that had burnt the ground on which his village once stood down to the rock.

He will be hung tomorrow at dawn. But he has been granted the favour of being allowed before dying to speak a last poem before the people.

★

He said to himself in his cell:
Until now I've only made poems to amuse myself.
This will be my first and last poem.
I shall say to them:
   – Take these words, so that they may not become a lost seed!
   Incubate my words, make them grow, make them speak!
But what shall I say to them after that?
I've only one word to say to them, a word as simple as a thunderbolt.
A word that makes my heart swell, a word that ascends to my throat, a word that paces about in my head like a caged lion.

It is not a word of peace. It is not an easy word to understand.

But it ought to lead to peace, it ought to make all things easy to understand, provided it be taken as the earth receives the seed and nourishes it while killing it. When I shall have begun to rot, in a few days' time, may a word-bearing tree emerge from my rotting remains. Not words of peace, not easily understood words, but words of truth.

★

But still, what shall I say to them?

I have only one word to say, a word as real as the rope with which I shall be hanged.

A word that irks me, a word that consumes me,

a word that even the hangman will be able to understand.

I shall open my mouth – I shall say the word – I shall shut my mouth – and that will be all.

As soon as I've opened my mouth there will be seen going back to their place underground the vampires and all the purloiners of words, the cheats at the game of living, death's speculators:

Those who go in for table-turning,

those who swing pendulums,

those who search amongst the stars for reasons not to do anything.

The idle dreamers, the suicides,

those with a mania for mystery,

those with a mania for pleasure,

the imaginary travellers, cartographers of thought,

those with a mania for the arts who don't know why they're singing, dancing, painting or building.

Those with a mania for the beyond

who don't know how to be here below.

Those with a mania for the past, a mania for the future, pilferers of eternity.

They will be seen going back underground as soon as I've opened my mouth.

As soon as I've uttered the word, the eyes of the survivors will turn round in their sockets, and each one of those men and women will look the extremity of their fate in the face.

Gulf of light! Dolorous darkness!

As soon as I've shut my mouth, their eyes, suffused with the central light, will turn back to the world, and they will see that the outer is as the image of the inner.

/ René Daumal

They will be kings, they will be queens, they will see one another, each one alone as the sun is alone, but all illumined by the fire of a single inner solitude, as without by the fire of a single sun.

★

But I am dreaming and yielding to too easy a hope.
Rather, no doubt – they will say:
    – That madman, it's time he was hanged. It's time that useless mouth was shut. Or even perhaps they will say:
    – His words are not words of peace, they are not words easy to understand. They are the words of an evil spirit. It's time to hang him.
And in any case I shall be hanged. Very well, I shall say to them:
    – You haven't much longer to live than I have.
I die today, you next week.
And our tribulation is the same and our greatness is the same.
But they will believe these to be words of hatred.
    These unfortunate creatures are so sure of being immortal.
    And in any case I shall be hanged.
What shall I say to them? I shall say to them clearly: Wake up! –
    but I shan't be able to tell them how to and they will say:
    – But we're not asleep. Hang him, hang this impostor
    and may his tongue be seen jerking out!
And I shall in any case be hanged.

★

And the poet, in his prison, battered his head against the wall. The sound of muffled drum-beats, the funereal tapping of his head against the wall was his penultimate song.
    All night long he tried to tear the unspeakable word out of his heart. But the word swelled up in his breast and surged to his throat and kept pacing round in his head like a caged lion.
    He repeated to himself:
In any case I shall be hanged at dawn.
    And he started once more the dull drumming of his head against the wall. Then he tried again:
There would be only one word to say. But that would be too simple.
They would say:
    – We know already. Hang, hang that driveller.
Or else they would say:
    – He wants to tear us away from the peace of our hearts, from our

only refuge in these calamitous times. He wants to put lacerating doubt into our heads, when the invader's whip is already lacerating our skins.

These are not words of peace, these are not easy words to understand.

Hang this malefactor, hang him!
And in any case I shall be hanged.
What shall I say to them?

★

The sun rose with the sound of boots. He was led, with clenched teeth, towards the gallows. Before him his brothers, behind him his executioners. Inwardly he said to himself:

So here is my first and last poem. Just one word to say, simple as opening one's eyes. But this word is eating me up from the belly to the head, I wish I could open myself up from the belly to the head and show them the word I contain. But if it has to be made to pass through my mouth, how will it venture through so narrow an orifice, this word with which I'm replete?

Then he held his tongue a first time: his mouth preserved silence. A second time he held his tongue: his heart closed up. A third time he held his tongue: his whole body became like a silent rock.

(He was like a white rock, like the statue of a ram before a flock of sleeping sheep; and behind him the wolves were already grinning).

★

The sounds of bayonets and spurs were to be heard. The granted reprieve came to an end. The poet felt on his neck the tickling of hemp and in the pit of his stomach the taloned paw of death. And then, at the last moment, the utterance burst forth from his mouth, vociferating:

To arms! To your pitchforks and knives,
To your stone missiles, your hammers,
you're a thousand, you're strong,
free yourselves, free me!
I want to live, live with me!
kill with scythe-strokes, kill with volleys of stones!
Accomplish my survival and I will restore your speech to life.

19

But that was his first and last poem.

The people were already far too terrorized.

And as he swung too much this way and that during his life, so is he still swinging after his death.

Under the feet of his corpse ripening on the bough the little devourers of carrion lie in wait. Above his head wheels his last cry, which has nobody on whom to perch.

(For it is often the fate – or the fault – of poets to speak too late or too soon).

Yves de Bayser (b. 1920)

A SELECTION OF POEMS FROM *INSCRIRE*

(1)
stars, you loved your names
the sky was at your bedsides, the famine of the fire

holidays lit up the snow
we governed the summer we
learnt to lie to cure
terror of song
we heard the storm destroy itself

to you, nightingales of the eclipse, grass
the beaten track, fragility
the scarecrow dies upon
the fields of fine weather and rain

saved up, you will grow old no more

(3)
numerous sweet dangerous hands
consort, when the day wandered we
wrote to rooms, edge of roads
motionless in the immense and painted air
wherein stars of less size than our hands
let the lightning-flash be touched and the page torn

(5)
at the foot of the tree at the stone's knees
in all the sounds of the daylight in
the night that I still find
it's written, that's certain: I want to die
she is that is not death

I write to dreams to their own dreams
the lying-in-wait place sets up the encampments
    of the moon
my dog my anxious soul
a cry awakes you at the moment of death
and the question is answer the inquiry protests

the days and the roads rush up
the non-poet lives in a dream

(10)

the non-poet lives in a dream

at my request,
it was that delicious suffering, a reverie of the years
just past

thrown down like myself, by the sleep of the master and exemplar,
the fellow beings, the nomads, the miracles reach the plain, remove
the limits, the frontiers, the fronts, push back the horizon, dispel the
flight, pursue the empire

beyond the ramparts, there is the suppression of free procedure, the
walls leaning against the walls along the walls like children, the
image of the walls around the walls, around the dwelling, around the
guard-dog, around the giant dwarf, around a snake, on the edge of
the alley, near the crevasse, how one is born a poet
nothing predisposed me to live

the voice said: last-born of the images, born-assassinated, they are
your bright hearth, your franchise, your brood and your blood,
gratitude to fire now dead, and knowledge of astonishment, wound
of a horse and the diamond's flaw, if the way on the warren was your
road, a piece of game would tremble in the kerchief, your brother
the scholar, brother treasurer, brother astronomer gratifies and
consoles, oh my guest, I am stronger than you, you will forget me,
you will forget the individual at the corner of the street, at the corner
of the woods, in the eyes, in the games, near the familiar stars, close
to the most familiar, the extreme end of a tress of hair

(11)

precursor

truly, he stands no more on my left, upright, proud, illiterate, hallucinated, drunk with a gift, that of courage

I do not know if the seasons were our parents, they were thirsty, they were hungry, I implored the darkness from the dark, and under the fleece of a passport, I stumbled in the eyes of the civilizing street, the lizard, who's afraid of fear

more or less as in days gone by at the moment of expiry, the soaring flight of fear, vigour and due time

today the tormented one, the well-being of one of the nightmares, the healthy appearance of beauty, proclaims the exorcist

cousin, from the words you use for thirst, I recognize the breach of the first steps, the private future of sleep, I am at last, my lord, your all-powerful distress

(17)

often

my brother speaks: I used to dislike daytime
whoever esteems me will have guessed the fact
a young girl wept
I hated a bird the night hated
at least I believed the night to be a portrait of my life
when the sky and its children slept
(the rose forgives and everything is forgotten)
countries passed by and knew me
immortal residents
oh the trace of your steps the fog and the stars of your guns
I go towards my brother with words that have been renounced
like the name of the day and many such days
of gods without demons and demons devoid of gods

there was a bird, my brother spoke of it sometimes

/ *Yves de Bayser*

(18)

already

the dawn is going to fetch the dawn
on the wrong side of our roads,
in the outburst of its praise
the day brings weddings painted
for a feast

we have discussed it with the poets
in the pampered and devoured towns,
we have talked about the hills and the water
above all about the transparency one can hear
I am the stone desiring the stone
the nights will have to leave you
they must never be unmindful of me
the suns will issue from me
without their arms without their empires
with fire and with festival,
fire the lost child
victim of the great trees
of their men's tales

(19)

conquest

the sea was entrusted to us as a torrent
a crazy act to liberate the sand
our homeland: gong of the forests
adores sand knees and hands
O gasping to our wooden wits
we thought of the sea of its body of its groove
we dreamed of it lying down in coils
ravaged by a torrent

(22)
to inscribe
a walker
a tracer
a landmark
a zero
walled up in the infinite
in a word

FROM PART II: *LA PORTE DES TRAITRES*

(1)
speaking writing: there you are, you
you are a king
and a people
in your own place
between a heavy river
and stairs of stone
in another abode
behind your gate
and before you

portal of a tower
all the regal and all the rabble
on the widest and the least wide courtyard
like the ground and like the air

gate that is never passed through twice
gate of the face-to-face and the tête-à-tête

(5)
my king vanquished
by me
my song
I nourish him with all my might
the fire of the cold the fool of the sky
animals chased from surfeited lands

/ Yves de Bayser

(6)
tower perched on the highest tower
poetry is prison for ever
speech would be
speech or treason
perched on the highest tower
speech could be betrayed
and poetry would be
could be
treason of treason
contradiction of contradiction
torture of torture
oh the outcry the writing

(7)
you are, bits of the dream
bits of meat and of music
no partial truth
and that which is not true is veracious

the dream says
no one denies me
I am the dream
the exile the treason the rape
our numerous tongues
our timid tongues
our spiteful tongues
our unknown tongues
our foreign tongue
in our naked tongue

(13)
take away the dukes, convey nightbirds
close the iron, a staircase, an escalade
and the nightbirds will be your black birds

he comes from the river
trembling
because, O earth, of the river water
he walks with a firm step he has the easy gait
of the firm mad unreal and hard earth

the unreal our bread our daily memories
us: a powerful art, the fragile and the strong
jostle it and remain
place in the place and the other place
time within time and the other time

FROM PART III: *AMOUREUSE OBÉISSANCE ET CROYANCE*

(3)
sometimes the flowers are strangers, sometimes life is sweet, and
death sweet also, sometimes we wish for an immense misfortune, a
reconciliation with death, sometimes I like to say it in cadence,
addressing myself to music, addressing myself to those who hear so
exactly the will of words, their refrains, across the frontiers and the
musics of the nations of poetry, and I love, above all I love to say:
I love you because God has willed that I love you. He, serious as a
tender and respectful child, has kissed your cheek and says to your
lover: 'oh breath, oh breath of breath, you are his friend, his husband,
his lover, as yet it's only raining on the country of the image' music
listens so attentively . . . God does not wish to destroy, God breathes

(7)
oh, tormented by hands
she lays hands, perhaps yours, on the meadow
among the shadows of the sun
it is the desert its thirst the amorous landmarks
and then the lightning and then the storm

to offer you drink, oh rain
I'm athirst of quenching you as
the snake-charmer of the lightning
renders to gentleness blow for blow

then the star teaches the dark
the friendship of a peril: the air

(17)
you keep close to the rampart of inspired things,
to the walls that are the dream's muscles you
dare to say: only sleep dies
the dream stammers: poetry poetry and truth
God must absolutely must breathe
in words which roam over the earth
of the wild sun and moon
infinite infirm unthinkable always

(18)

to Clorette

laugh, we see no reason to
in the flames of paradise
I advance slowly, our irreality
I approach the reality of dreams
when approaching walls
I love you, you are frail, God is the frailest
oh curtain of poetry
God is the most frail

Robert Desnos (1900 – 45)

THERE WAS A LEAF

There was a leaf with all its lines
Line of life
Line of luck
Heart line
There was a branch at the end of the leaf
Forked line sign of life
Sign of luck
Heart sign
There was a tree at the end of the branch
A tree deserving life
Deserving luck
Deserving heart
Engraved, pierced and run through heart,
A heart that no-one ever saw.
There were roots at the end of the tree
Roots vines of life
Vines of luck
Heart vines
At the roots' ends there was the earth
Nothing but the earth
The earth all round
The earth all alone across the sky
The earth.

André du Bouchet (b.1924)

CABLE

The thick rope of country days
has bound me
I wear myself out
covered with a carapace of iron
and like me
the day has closed
my wound
buried
the diagonal band
of trees
and the air
laid by
which made us shiver
the earth's surface
I am deaf
and smooth
I don't understand the words of the tree
which continues to talk from time to time
above the bath-tub
put out in the field
like a cold trough
from which the day will have emerged

entirely

Paul Eluard (1895 – 1952)

ONE FOR ALL

One or many
The sky lying on the storm
The birds covered with snow
The sounds of fear in the harsh woods

One or many
Ravens are laid in shells of clay
With faded wings and landslide beaks
They have gathered the red fantastic roses of the storm

One or many
The collars of the sun
The sun's immense strawberry
On the bottleneck of a grove

One or many
More sensitive to their childhood
Than to rain or fine weather
Sweeter to know
Than sleep on sweet slopes
Far from ennui

One or many
In whining mirrors
Where their voices are torn in the morning
Like linen

One or many
Made of crumbling stone
And of scattering feather
Made of cloth alcohol froth
Of laughter sobbing negligence ridiculous torments
Made of flesh and of unmistakable eyes

One or many
With all their woman's faults
All their merits

One or many
The face tightly covered with ivy
Tempting as new bread
All the women who rouse me
Dressed in what I have desired
Dressed in calm and freshness
Dressed in salt, water, sunlight
Tenderness audacity and a thousand caprices
In a thousand chains

One or many
In all my dreams
A new woodland flower
Barbaric flower with bundles of pistils
Which open in the burning circle of its deliriums
In the murdered night

One or many
A youth to die of
A violent unquiet youth saturated with ennui
In which she has taken part with me
Not caring for others.

THE SHEEP

Close your eyes black face
Close the gardens of the street
Intelligence and hardiness
Ennui and tranquillity
These sad evenings at every moment
The glass and the glass door
Comforting and sensible
And light, the fruit-tree
The flowering tree the fruit-tree
Fly away.

'AT THE END OF A LONG VOYAGE'

At the end of a long voyage I always see this corridor once more, this mole, this warm shadow to which the foam of the sea prescribes pure breezes like tiny children, I always see once more the room where I came to break with you the bread of our desires, I always see once more your undressed pallor which unites in the morning with the disappearing stars. I know I am going to close my eyes again in order to rediscover the colours and conventional forms which allow me to approach you. When I open them again it will be so as to find in a corner of the room the corruptible pickaxe-sleeved parasol which causes me to doubt fine weather, the sun, life, for I no longer love you in full daylight, I regret the time when I was setting out to discover you, and also the time when I was blind and dumb before the incomprehensible universe and the incoherent system of agreement that you were suggesting to me.

Have you not sufficiently borne the responsibility of that frankness which obliged me to be continually turning your own whims against you?

What haven't you given me to think about? I now come no longer to see you except in order to reassure myself of the great mystery which still constitutes the absurd duration of my life, the absurd duration of a night.

The boats all sail away when I arrive, the storm recoils before them. A shower sets free the obscure flowers, their blossoming begins again and strikes once more the woollen walls. You are never sure of anything, I know, but the idea of falsehood and the idea of an error are so much stronger than we are. It is so long since the obstinate door refused to give in, so long since the monotony of hope fed boredom, so long since your smiles were tears.

We have refused to allow spectators to enter, for there is nothing to see. Remember, when you are alone, the empty stage without any scenery or actors or musicians. Thus it is: the theatre of the world, the worldly stage, and we two, we no longer know what it means. We two – I insist on those words, for at the ports of call on those long voyages we made separately, I know it now, we were really together, we really were, we were, we. Neither you nor I know how to add the time when we were apart to the time when we were together, neither you nor I know how to take one away from the other.

Each one a shadow, but in the shadow we forgot that it was so.

33   / Paul Eluard

WHAT THE WORKMAN SAYS
IS NEVER TO THE POINT

A winter all branchy and hard as a corpse
A man on a bench in a street that escapes from the crowd
And is filled up with solitude
Makes way for the banal machinery of despair
For its mirrors of lead
For its baths of pebbles
For its stagnant statues
Makes way for the neglect of good
For the tattered memories of truth
Black light old conflagration
With hair lost in a labyrinth
A man who mistook the landing the door and the key
So as to know more so as to love more.

Where does the landscape begin
At what time
Where then does woman come to an end
The evening balances over the town
The evening rejoins the stroller in his bed
The naked stroller
Less greedy for a virgin breast
Than for the shapeless star that gives suck to the night.

There are indescribable demolitions sadder than a farthing
But nevertheless the sun escapes from them singing
While the sky dances and makes its honey
There are deserted walls where the idyll blossoms
Where the flaking plaster
Cradles mingled shadows
A rebellious fire a fire of veins
Beneath the only wave of lips
Take hands see eyes
Take the landscape by force

Behind the palace behind the rubbish-heaps
Behind the chimneys and the cisterns
In front of man
On the esplanade that unrolls a coat of dust
By fever drawn

It is the invasion of fine days
A plantation of blue daggers
Beneath the opened eyelids in a crowd of leaves
It is pleasure's heavy harvest.

The flower of flax breaks the masks
The faces are washed
By the colour that knows the extent.

The clear days of the past
Their barred lions and their eagles of pure water
Their thunder of pride inflating the hours
With the blood of enchained dawns
All across the sky
Their diadem shrivelled on the mace of a single mirror
Of a single heart.

But now far deeper among the abolished roads
This song that holds the night
This song that deafens and blinds
That offers its arms to ghosts
This denying love
That struggles in anguish
With well-soaked tears
This torn disabled twisted ridiculous dream
This fallow harmony
This begging horde.

For she has desired only gold
And love's perfection
Her whole life long.

/ Paul Eluard

STATEMENT

Poetry is not necessarily limited by the secret ideas you have about it. But like the dreams one does not tell, it is apt to cause lapses of memory and to prevent the regular formation of a world superior to that in which forgetfulness is used for the self-preservation of the individual.

That inspiration may leap freely from the mirror, all reflections of the personality must be effaced. Give influences free play, invent what has already been invented, what is beyond doubt, what is unbelievable, give spontaneity its pure value. Be the man who is questioned and who is heard. A single vision, infinitely varied.

THE POET IS HE WHO INSPIRES FAR MORE THAN HE WHO IS INSPIRED.

from *LIKE AN IMAGE*

Armour of prey the black perfume shines
Trees wear an almond landscape hair
Cradle of all the landscapes the keys of dice
The plains of care and mountains of alabaster
The lamps of the suburbs, bashfulness, storms
Unforeseen gestures devoted to fire
The paths separating the sea from its drowned
All the undecipherable riddles.

The thistle flower builds a castle
It climbs the ladders of the wind
And death's head seeds.
Ebony stars on the glistening panes
Promise all to their lovers
The others who pretend
Maintain the leaden order.

Silent misery of man
His early morning face
Opens like a prison
His eyes are heads cut off

Paul Eluard /   36

His fingers serve to count
To measure to take to convince
His fingers know how to bind him.

Ruin of the public
Its emotion is in tatters
Its enthusiasm damped
The ornaments suspended to the terrors of thunder
Livid pastures where rocks leap out
To put an end to it
A tomb adorned with the prettiest trinkets
A silken veil over the languor of lust
To put an end to it
With a single blow of an axe in the back.

In the ravines of sleep
Silence rears its children
Here is the fatal sound that bursts the ear-drums
The dusty death of colours
Idiocy
Here is the first idler
And the unconscious movements of insomnia
The ear the reeds to curve back like a helmet
The exacting ear the enemy forgotten in the mist
And the inexhaustible silence
Which overthrows nature by not naming it
Which sets up smiling snares
Of frightening absences
Breaks all the mirrors of the lips.

On the open sea in delicate arms
On fine days the waves in full sail
And the blood leads to everything
It is a square without a statue
Without rowers without a black flag
A rainbow-coloured naked square
Where all the wandering flowers
Flowers at the mercy of the light
Have concealed fairylands of daring
It is a jewel of indifference
Within the scope of every heart
The chiselled jewel of laughter

/ Paul Eluard

It is a mysterious house
Where children baffle men
On the outskirts of hope
To no purpose
Calm creates a vacuum

★

Revolt of the snow
Soon falling back beneath a single stroke of dark
Just time to near the oblivion of the dead
To make the earth turn pale.
On the steps of torrents
Cool-browed crystal girls
Small girls who blossom and weak girls who smile
To announce the water seduce the light.

Sunset and liquid dawns

And when their kisses become invisible
They go to sleep between the lions' jaws.

★

I leave the caves of anguish
And the slow curves of fear
I fall into a well of down
I had never dreamed I should find you
Poppies again
In a closed mirror
You are as beautiful as fruit
And so heavy O my masters
That you must need wings to live
Or else my dreams.

Childhood stays at home
To blush for its duties
To be worthy of life
With its games of all colours
Its shorn books and its acid pencil-boxes
A hand closes and settles in repose
A child's hands
Like frogs.

But see how the arrogant dust
Rises and falls and shuffles
Bodiless full of charms
All stripped and strange
A palace welcomes and receives it accompanies it
With its façade with the great first book
With the keys that offend the walls
The raised curtains of the smile
To delude us into believing that wrinkles
Do not measure the threefold interior.

The lizard's shortest track
Upsets all precautions
The wood's smallest death
When the axe cuts the thread
And sets free a bird
Surprise's beating wings.

Armature of the freckled – bright adornment
And this mistrust of all underground plants
For blessing the poisons for honouring the fevers
The springs are crowned with shade
The body shares its conquests
But its youth is concealed.

Renounce O poppies
The difficult journey of seeds.

ALL THE RIGHTS

Simulate
The flowered shadow of flowers hung from spring
The shortest day of the year and the esquimau night
The agony of autumnal visionaries
The odour of roses the wise stinging of nettles
Stretch transparent linen
Into the clearing of your eyes
Display the ravages of fire its works of inspiration

/ Paul Eluard

And the paradise of its ash
The abstract phenomenon struggling with the clock's hands
The wounds of truth the oaths that cannot fold
Display yourself

You can go in crystal robes
Your beauty goes on and on
Your eyes shed tears caresses smiles
Your eyes have no secrets
And are limitless.

ARP

Turns unreflecting to the smileless curves of bearded shadows, registers the murmurs of speed, the diminutive terror, searches beneath the cold cinders for the smallest birds, those that never fold their wings, resists the wind.

NECESSITY

Without great ceremony on earth
Near those who keep their poise
On this misery of all repose
Right near the good way
In the dust of the serious
I establish relations between man and woman
Between the smeltings of the sun and the bag of bees
Between the enchanted grottoes and the avalanche
Between the care-rimmed eyes and the pealing laughter
Between the heraldic blackbird and the star of garlic
Between the leaden thread and the sound of the wind
Between the fountain of ants and the growing of strawberries
Between the chalcedony and winter in pins
Between the eye-ball tree and the recorded mimicry

Between the carotid and the ghost of salt
Between the auracaria and the head of a dwarf
Between the branching rails and the speckled dove
Between man and woman
Between my solitude and you.

AT PRESENT

For a long time without songs
Flowers cultivated flowers for sale
O beautiful abstract virtues

Washing is in vain one no longer sees oneself
Quietly sleeping in a bed of ashes
Under shelter of all the morrows

There is no way out
No more daylight between the houses
A cockroach sleeps on every sill
Content has taken death for sign

The stunningly charming young
And the old in their stinking chains
How alike they are!
The others awaken in spite of them
Their brows and their bellies are wrinkled
But fire still draws them on

Out of touch with everything save misery
Alert, they would rather not believe
In the immobility of their blood.

/ *Paul Eluard*

CRITIQUE OF POETRY

Of course I hate the reign of the bourgeois
The reign of cops and priests
But I hate still more the man who does not hate it
As I do
With all his might

I spit in the face of that despicable man
Who does not of all my poems prefer this *Critique of Poetry*

A WOMAN

   I have fallen from my fury, fatigue disfigures me, but still I see
you, burning women, mute stars, I shall see you forever, madness.
   And thou, the blood of the stars flows in thee, their light sustains
thee. On the flowers, thou standest upon the flowers, on the stones
with the stones.
   Dead whiteness of memories, exposed, starred, radiant with thy
tears which flow. I am lost.

GEORGES BRAQUE

A bird flies away,
It discards the clouds like a useless veil,
It has never feared the light,
Enclosed in its flight,
It has never owned a shadow.

Shells of harvests broken by the sun.
All the leaves in the woods say yes,
They know only how to say yes,
Every question, every reply
And the dew flows in the depths of this yes.

Paul Eluard /   42

A man with roving eyes describes the sky of love.
He gathers its wonders
Like leaves in a wood,
Like birds in their wings
And men in their sleep.

GIORGIO DE CHIRICO

A wall denounces another wall
And the shadow defends me from my timid shadow
O circling of my love around my love,
All the walls spun whitely round my silence.

And what were you defending? Heartless and pure sky,
Trembling you shielded me. The light in relief
Against the sky that mirrors no more the sun,
The daytime stars among green leaves,

The memory of those who spoke unknowingly,
Masters of my weakness whose place is now my own
With eyes of love and far too faithful hands
To bereave a world from which I am absent now.

From *Capitale de la Douleur* (1924)

ANDRÉ MASSON

Cruelty ties itself up and nimble gentleness unties itself. The magnet of wings draws faces very close, the flames of the earth make their escape by the breasts and the jasmin of hands unfolds about a star.

The torpid sky, the sky that dedicates itself is no longer over us.

/ *Paul Eluard*

Oblivion, better than evening, effaces it. Deprived of blood and reflections, the cadence of the temples and the columns is maintained.

The lines of the hand are so many branches in the whirling wind. Stair-flight of the winter months, day's pallor of insomnia, but also, in the shadow's most secret rooms, a body's garland wreathed about its splendour.

BEAUTY AND RESEMBLANCE

A face at the end of the day
A cradle in the day's dead leaves
A bouquet of naked rain
Every sun hidden
Every spring springs in the water's depths
Every mirror of broken mirrors
A face in the scales of silence
A pebble among pebbles
For the fronds of the last glimmers of day
A face like all the forgotten faces.

POETIC OBJECTIVITY

only exists in the succession, the linking together of all the subjective elements of which the poet, until the beginning of the new order, is not the master but the slave.

War of wanderers and guides
Contrary to apprehensions
Contrary to advice
Far from the most sensitive shores
To fly from the salubrious seas
Hope's early endeavours
To fly from the inhuman colours
Tempests with lifeless gestures
And great empty bodies
The labyrinth of exiled stars

The oceans of milk and wine and meats
The waves of fur and the waves of sleep
The sand in its bed
To fly from the ships and their appointed tasks

VOID

He puts a bird on the table and closes the shutters.
He combs his hair and it is lovelier in his hands
than a bird.

She says it is coming. And I am meant to verify it.

The bruised heart, the aching soul, the broken hands,
the white hair, the prisoners, all waters are upon me
like an open wound.

A PERSONALITY ALWAYS NEW

Knives so sharp and so strong as to lose all their weight
Flashing in the thick of the struggling crowd the most tired and the
    most proud
Knives like statues of fury
Like hunters on the tracks of filthy tramps
Knives like ultimate stars,
Like prison bars in the wind
Knives to weep and never weep again
Knives to attack the flowered paper of dawn
To demolish the foundations of life black and white like a loaf
Knives like a glass of poison on the breath
Like the bare arms of a dazzling mourning
Watching over the agony of floods

In order to know the end of the absurd.

(fragment)

/ *Paul Eluard*

HUMPHREY JENNINGS

Under a black sky black houses burnt-out embers
And you with hard head
Consenting mouth
Moist hair
Sturdy roses in your blood
Despairing of an endless fair dark day
You break the frozen colours
You disturb the diamond's track
An amber boat with three oars
Excavates the desert's pond
The wind sprawls on the foam
An entire evening sustains the dawn
Movement has roots
Stillness expands and blossoms.

1938

'YESTERDAY'S CONQUERORS SHALL PERISH'

Front de fer front de singe
Ils perdront de vue la mer

1
A sheep lies rotting on the slag
The trees lend hue and freshness to the hanged
The day's rough diamonds polish the hard blood

2
Their dreams were not of filling up their grave
Of going down in mud

3
In the land of masters nothing grows but fire

4

A bitter face
Of blue milk and black honey
Gathered in fever
A face that's unashamed
With widely opening eyes
As living as a race of men
And sure to keep watch come what may

5

In those unhappy eyes grows only fire

6

Keeping close watch, arousing fear
Causing to give up, winning more warmth for the heart

7

But our desires are not so ardent in the night
My brothers, as this bright red star
Which gains ground on the horror despite all.

14 April 1938

DEATH OF A MONSTER

You must keep watch for your approaching death
To be aware you're still alive
So high the risen tide, your heart so low
Son of the soil, eater of flowers, fruit of the burnt-out fire
Darkness blots out for evermore all sky within your breast.

The sun lets go the string and the walls' dances cease
Sunlight abandons to the birds those lanes where none may pass.

/ Paul Eluard

HUNTED

A few grains of dust more or less
On ancient shoulders
Locks of weakness on weary foreheads
This theatre of honey and faded roses
Where incalculable flies
Reply to the black signs that misery makes to them

Despairing girders of a bridge
Thrown across space
Thrown across every street and every house
Heavy wandering madnesses
That we shall end by knowing by heart
Mechanical appetites and uncontrolled dances
That lead to the regret of hatred

Nostalgia of justice

SISTERS OF HOPE

Sisters of hope O you courageous women
Against death you have made a pact
The pact consolidating all the virtues love has

O my sisters who've survived
You stake your lives
That life may triumph in the end

O my sisters of true greatness the day is near
When we shall laugh at the words war and poverty
And everything causing your sorrow will have collapsed
When every face will make good its claim to be kissed.

MAX ERNST

At the age of life
Everything flung away everywhere
Everything seemed incongruous
A bottle of excellent syrup a bunch of violets
There are some of every kind
Inoffensive pebbles a strikingly lifelike lake
The forehead pressed against the wall follows the clouds
Now's not the time when all hope's dead
There's more time left
The eyes extinguished by the tedious day glitter as evening falls.

*When the monster felt himself struck he ascribed the face to overseer like a
man in a state of rage who'd wanted to call out.*
His courage had grown dull.
Then the second and third wind-balloon come.
Witticism – It's better not to reward a good action at all than to reward it ill.
A soldier had lost both arms in a battle. His colonel offered him an écu. *The
soldier answered him: You believe, no doubt,* mon colonel, *that I've only
lost a pair of gloves.*
The ear at the bottom of humourless heads
Penmanship his happiness

The letter disfigures the word

The nudity of woman is wiser than the philosopher's teaching.
It doesn't demand to be pondered.
Whistles cries whisperings
Buds of anger parings of laughter
Mingled with hand-claps in the interceding window-panes
Overburden the nudity of the heart's long heavy chains.

As a bird stretches out in the smoke
The recall of plain speech
Tremblingly traces foliations of charms
Embroideries of flesh volleys of movements
The delight of going towards forgotten beings
Along unforgettable paths.

From *La Vie Immédiate* (1932)

/ *Paul Eluard*

BALTHUS

The petty hassles of spoilt children
Soon smirch the green amongst the furze
And the incorruptible sand falls out of skirts
Rain will no longer launder these hell-cats' pelts for them

For her defective plaited brats the mother
Built like a bucket will never have hard words
But will dress them up in golden lace
Begging in Paradise she bids their bodies come

Soiled rags protecting the egg in the valley
The dwarf flame loses its flower in the mirror
And this laugh is the end of laughter for ever
And this source is the first and the last as well

To see the end of a dream in which games were still being played
See the grave yawn ahead and the flesh gain weight
Both on the earth and beneath it the children are now forgotten
A drop of blood makes the universe grow dark.

Pierre Emmanuel (1916 – 84)

ASIA

The plains subdued under the yoke drag on and on
Beneath the biting sea-winds' whip like worn out beasts.
Asia! ah, all thy ivory-hued horizons, thy enormous realms
Left lying there like mummies 'midst the shrivelled parchment wastes.'
The intermittent whinneying down the ages of thy cries –
Lament like that of straying fowls for all thy heights laid low!
Where is Palmyra, gold and jade beneath her palms?
Where now do the proud cedars of blue Lebanon lie stretched?
Those left still standing cast no shade on flocks for they are dead,
And stripped of leaves and honeycombs are those great glades,
I have seen towns spurred by the lash of raging suns,
Cut by the branding-iron in squares beneath a sky of flint,
Spawning like clouds of star-dust locust swarms
Eager to eat through glass or marble: A whole night
Passed by. The ruined dawn was thousands of years old. The very
        black
Earth was in mourning for a score of dusty tribes.

Jean Follain (1903 – 71)

SOME POEMS FROM *PRÉSENT JOUR*

1.   *THE BIRD ON THE BREASTS*

At the ford crossed by night
at this graceful outline of bodies
mounting the steps of ruined houses
a scared dream struggles
crossed by the lain-down breasts of women
on which the shadow of branches stirs
and on these surfaces of flesh
using up their duration
vivaciously a bird
sings and treads
in the hour that's striking.

2.   *EMPTY SUIT*

Empty suit at the bottom of a cellar
badly resists wearing out all alone
enveloped in damp
prey to blind little insects
it loses its colours from one day to the next
nobody thinks that God can see it
in the atrocious and sweet universe
in its unchanging place.

3.   *PRESENT DAY*

In the present day
people flee
biting right into bread
the clouds change form
in the low sky

a shivering of branches
gives rise to dreaming better or worse
a door opening onto the lane
shows a face
and two hands
one of them wearing a ring
the rest of the body is wrapped
in an unaged sheet.

4.   *ONLY SON*

When ruined evening falls
with wind in the tall grasses
it's no longer any kind of time,
for her with the black neckerchief
tied across her breast
her beauty hasn't been made up
at the hour when it ought to have been
a shadow lies at her feet
the blooms called sunflowers sway to and fro
with eyes tired from gazing
she awaits her only son
each step of the stairs will groan
one more time
beneath her scaly shoes.

5.   *WORDS*

Bearers of suffering
certain words
rejoin the silences of death
those of the bearers of boughs
and of the soldier
who finds a key under the snow.
Sun lighting the forests of old trees
forests where vivid flowers are growing
participate in the contours of worlds.
In the hamlets
as in the enormous building-blocks
people talk about sacrifices for love.

6.   *SPACE REMAINS*

There remains unusable space
where the object sinks
in a faint sound of reeds.
One must always pick up one's steps long or short
one after another on the twisting road.
Sometimes one man says to another
stop listening, shut up, don't move
so that time may stand still
and not go away again across the stars.

7.   *STRUCTURES OF TIME*

Where will you go when you're dead says the master
everyone replies to heaven
from the suit falls a button
that will have to be sewn on again this evening
the stone flung by hatred
falls far from the man aimed at
one sees structures shining
that the coming night will mingle
waves cover up
silent sand-castles.
According to the saying of Heraclitus
time seems like a playing child
the fine days full of bird-song
pass swiftly into eternity.

8.   *CONDEMNED*

Here's the condemned man his head cropped
but the roots of the hair
continue to feed themselves
in order to grow again for him
his ruddy fleece
blood makes his ears purple
no more woman

washing his throat with black soap
hands stretched out towards a radiating bowl
then the oaks tremble
and the evening clouds scud along in silence.

9. *PREY OF THE DREAM*

Adam means blood-vapour
a man thinks of it one peaceful day
but also of the future that he'll never see
a plait comes undone
in the hair of an oval-faced woman
who's promised herself to stay awake
but has fallen asleep in her chair
full of shadows and curves
with pigments on her skin
a prey to the dream of her slow life.

10. *A GREEN CORNER*

Sometimes an animal stays behind
gentle and sad in a green corner
no-one knows
where she comes from
a sound of foliage scares her
with her clawed pads
she tramples a tiny flower
without seeing it
then night covers everything up again.

11. *THE LAND OF PUMAS*

In the land of pumas
Indians talk to one another in a hollowed-out place
near a rock which seems
an empty-eyed face
all nuances becomes fixed at daybreak
from a tumbledown hovel a soot-coloured pig emerges

in the evening the earth stains itself with blood
from the sunset of the Andes
with the altitude
the night-rain will no longer hear itself.

12.   *SOMEONE'S RINGING*

Someone's ringing
says the child, someone's ringing
yet the snow's falling
on emaciated trees
the embers are dying out
a young girl in the blonde room
grew up to be atrociously lovely
images go round within her
the door's not opened
to whoever's still ringing the bell.

13.   *HATS*

Somewhere somebody rediscovers
an English cape of corroded leather
like the one which Lenin
scrubbed with petrol
before straddling his bike with its little bell.
It's wearing a shiny top-hat
that the banker Jecker
during the Commune walks to his death
talking about his Mexican tactics
to the officer in charge of the firing-squad.
In the world you see
worn-out felt hats
and their owners sitting down
near the statues
of great men or gods.

14. *SILENT FILMS*

She was already old the first time she saw
moving pictures
in a darkened hall
bread took on for her another taste
the nails of her wide-open hands were different
and the dust-motes in the air;
no doubt she was too elderly
for it to have seemed to her to have changed
that picture of God
on façades and porticos
on full days just as at every twilight.

15. *MEMORIAL*

The Ansaris have the cult of dogs
they preserve their skeletons
dried and whitened
by the ravaging heat-waves;
the old orange trees
on a hill-side turning blue
bear learnèd names
upon their trunks.
The dogma of man's divinity
continues to be observed.

16. *BROKEN BOTTLE*

Buildings close in the landscape
in the foreground are piles of wood
seated dreamers
and on the ground
the dark splinters
of the bottle lying there broken since a year ago
when a sudden disturbance
made someone drop it after singing a love-song.

17.   NOTCHES

The schools' notched table
displays initials
the paths intermingle
round the granite building
a great dane barks
in the shadows vegetation grows emaciated
someone says:
I am old
in his hand run the same veins
that were in it in his childhood
laden with goods a ship leaves
the town and its rubbish.

18.   SEPARATIONS

In the climbing street
a door opens on a bed
dominated by a Christ on a black cross
the one who talked so much yesterday
has said nothing all day
memories lose shape
but the hands' movements continue
a fly crawls about
over a statue's torso
God is but love says a voice
the ashes are scattered
the home maintains its foundations
in spite of death.

19.   WOMEN WITH DARK CIRCLES
ROUND THEIR EYES

Dark circles round their eyes
there are those who marvel
that an Oriental poem
calls their body a vine.

They look at themselves
in the pond surrounded by trees
disappear down the centuries
in the pupil of the eye
of artisans and ageing tyrants.

20.   *THE MACHINE*

The idler sees some of the firmament
through the daylight let in by the shutter
one hears the sound of a machine
long used for the making of lined paper.
In the evening it stops
then rise the historic odours
of clay and stone village
blazing towns, red deserts,
creatures of flesh.

Benjamin Fondane (1898 – 1944)

POEM 1933

That girl was mad in that old village
all alone with herself and all alone in God
with her swollen breasts and living entrails,
who'd been awaiting for centuries, a guest
to come and take his place, on a stormy night, in her bed,
with the enormous rod of the Saints of Paradise.
While awaiting this day, she went to confession,
washed with much water her thighs and her buttocks,
and cared for with art the strange and crude place
that one evening the Elect would come to search out and visit.
One evening, while she lay asleep near her dirty dishes,
attracted by the powerful odour of her armpits,
a donkey entered the house. In horror,
she tried to cover up her nudity with a tear,
but her body was virgin, her soul was a believer's.
She controlled her fear, mastered her terror,
and understanding, suddenly, the obscure design of God,
she laid her body on the obsequious donkey
and experienced in a fantastic and hysterical spasm
the first metaphysical sensations.

TWO POEMS FROM *AU TEMPS DU POÈME, 1944*

I. *IS IT?...*

Is it a universe of ropes,
pulleys, masts and steam-funnels?
of old ship-sirens worn with runnels,
of ancient lacy window-drapes?

How many tired and patinous shades,
the damaged hostages of time,
turn with an absent-minded gaze
the gold book's pages, morns of days.

Shall we climb the gangway to the boat?
Its dense reflection biting the sea below
shakes in the eye which freezes it.

All in this scene's so wrapped in calm,
gnawed, O decay of the Selfsame,
by our nostalgia for the Extreme!

II. *SOMETIMES*

It sometimes happens that he's jealous of
the death of a fruit, the fall of a leaf,
the sound of a wounded word that will collect itself
before letting out a cry.

It sometimes happens that he must disturb
the water of a pool or of his face;
it's as though a god wished to reduplicate
– to prevent its flight – his likeness there.

Could man be alone in not knowing how
to leave things behind, caught by his roots,
like one who can scarcely still recall
that other country bordering his own?

Sometimes he also asks himself
whether it will be hard to disappear
without having been able in the water of things
to perfect the long reflection of a calm.

/ Benjamin Fondane

André Frenaud (1907 – 93)

BUT WHO'S AFRAID?

Drenched trees
weapons grown rusty,
stolen star,
torpid heart,
encircled horses,
vanished castle,
diminished forest,
abandoned access,
distraught verge,
dispossessed source

– the snow wears a smile.

Eugène Guillevic (b.1907)

MEMORY

In memory of Gabriel Péri

It's not true that a dead man
Is like a vague empire
Full of orders and noise,

That he envies us
When we eat.

It's not true that a dead man
Is higher at night from blood or milk than us.

It is not he who laughs in the tree and the wind
If somebody weeps in the village.

Nor is it he
Who makes the crockery fall when one's back is turned
Or soot on the fire

It's never a dead man
Who looks with hostility at us in young goats' eyes.

Never tell lies.
There's nothing so dead as a dead man.

– But it's true that the dead
Make a silence on earth
That's deeper than sleep.

From *Exécutoire*

Maurice Henry (1907 – 85)

THE BRONZE PIANO

If the hyenas whistled
to keep inclemencies away
if the vehicles played hide-and-seek with Poetry
if street-noises served glaciers as coat-pegs
the rivers would break up the ships
from end to end
hedgehogs would say mass in the music of rapes
the wounded men would not bleed so much
the acrobats would be undone
like phosphorus
one would kill oneself on station-approaches like crystals

And if the streams
recognized the veiled women who pass in the explosion of sparrows
the aeroplanes would go back under the earth like pen-holders
head first

With ifs
we would cut off the heads of kings and of motor-cycles
we would fight on the terraces of cafes why not
we would crowd out the pavements and even
prick ourselves with golden-horned lambs
with ifs
we would unchain torpedoes
syllables pebbles laughs
we would unchain the thieves and also the sewing-machines also the
     rats
the hearses would fly away before the cemetery

We are the pillows the mattresses the counterpanes
we are the sheets the blankets and the eiderdowns
and we are asleep
like post-cards.

Friedrich Hölderlin (1770 – 1843)

SONG OF DESTINY

Soft are your footsteps on the soft ground
In the great light, O peaceful Presences!
The shining winds of heaven
Lightly touch you
As the musician's fingers
Touch the sacred strings.

They have no destiny, the heavenly ones
Who breathe like a sleeping child.
And pure is in their keeping
The forever flowering mind.
And the blessed eyes gaze long
Within the clear eternal peace.

But never unto us was given
To repose.
Man in his suffering blindly falls
And vanishes again from hour to hour
Like waves against the breakwater
Flung to and fro into uncertainty through time.

THE HALF OF LIFE

Adorned with yellow pears
And with wild roses filled,
The earth hangs in the lake.
And wondrous love-intoxicated swans
In peaceful holy waters dip their heads.

My woe! When winter comes
Where shall I find the rose?
Where shall I find the sunshine and

The shadows of the earth?
The cold unspeaking walls rise up,
The flags flap in the wind.

AGES OF LIFE

O towns of the Euphrates!
And Palmyra's streets!
O forest of pillars on the desert plain
What are you?
                    When you passed
Beyond the limit of our breath,
Through the smoke of the heavenly Presences and through
The distant fires, your crowns
Were taken from you. Now
I sit beneath the clouds (of which
Each has its resting-place), beneath
The ordered oaks, amid
The wastelands of the roe;
And foreign to me and dead they seem,
The blessèd souls.

THE HARVEST

The ripe fruits are cast into the fire
And cooked, and tried upon the earth, and it is
A law
That everything returns to the within,
Thus spake the prophetic snakes which dream
Upon the hillsides of the sky. And there is much
Like a burden of wood upon the shoulders
To be preserved. The paths are treacherous.
And unordained
From side to side like horses pass

The prisoned Elements and old Principles of the Earth.
And a desire moves ever towards its free expression.
But there is much
To be preserved. And there is need of faith
But we do not wish to see both before and behind.
Or let ourselves rock
As in the frailest barque upon the sea.

PATMOS

The God is near, and
                           difficult to grasp.
But danger fortifies the rescuing power.
In sombre places dwell the eagles; the Alps' sons
Go fearless forth upon the roads of the abyss
Across lightly constructed bridges. And since all round there press
The peaks of time, and those so close
In love, are worn out on the separate heights,
Then give us the innocent waters,
O give us wings, that with the truest thought
We may fly yonder and return to this same place.

I spoke thus. And then rose
A guardian spirit, carried me away
More swiftly and still further than I dreamed.
Far from my house and home.
And as I passed, the light of dawn
Glowed on the shady woods and longed-for streams
Of my own land. I knew the earth no more.
And soon, with mysterious freshness shining
And rapidly growing beneath the footsteps of the sun,
In golden haze there blossomed forth
In a thousand peaks, a thousand glittering spires,

Asia, before my eyes. I blindly sought
For some familiar image,
A stranger to those wide streets where there descends
From Tmolus to the sea the Pactolus adorned with gold,

/ *Friedrich Hölderlin*

And the Taurus rises with Messogis,
And the flowering garden like a peaceful fire,
But in the light on high, the silver snow
And sign of immortal life, on the unscaled wall
The age-old ivy grows, and on living pillars
Of cedar and of laurel
Stand the solemn palaces the Gods have built.

And all around the Asiatic gates,
Calling out here and there from the sea's uncertain plain,
There murmur the unshadowed roads:
But the pilot knows the islands.
When I heard
That Patmos was among the nearest isles,
I longed to disembark
And to approach its gloomy caves
For it is not like Cyprus rich with springs
Or any of the other islands, it is not
In proud display that Patmos stands
But like a poor house full of hospitality,
And when from a wrecked ship, or weeping
For his lost land or for an absent friend
A stranger comes, she listens with good will;
And all her children, and the voices of the hot groves,
And the place where the sand falls, and where the fields are cracked
And all the sounds
Hear him, and all resounds again
With love for the man's plaint.
Thus it was one day that she took care
The belov'd of God, the seer
Who in his happy youth had gone

With the All-Highest's Son, inseparable from Him . . .

(Fragment)

'AND LITTLE KNOWLEDGE BUT MUCH PLEASURE'

And little knowledge but much pleasure
Is given to mortal men.

Why dost thou suffice me not O lovely sun
On this May day?
Thou flower of my flowers, what have I more than thee?

Would that I were as children are!
I should be like the nightingale were I to sing
All my delight in one enraptured song!

NATIVE LAND

And no one knows...

Yet let me walk
And gather the wild bays,
Expend my love for thee
O earth, upon thy roads,
Here where...
            ...and roses and their thorns
And the sweet limes send up their perfume from beside
The beechwood at noon, when the wild corn is alive
With whisper of the growth in its straight stalks
And its ears bend all one way
As to the autumn – Now beneath
The lofty swaying of the oaks,
When I reflect, when I interrogate the airs,
The sound of bells
                    I know so well
Sounding like gold, is heard afar.
It is the hour when the birds wake anew.
Then all is well.

PRINCE OF THE AIR

As the birds pass slowly by
The Prince gazes ahead
And happenings of the upper air
Are like cool breath against his breast
When there is silence round him
High above, but shining bright beneath
There lie the riches of the earth,
And with him go
In their first search for victory
The young.
But the Prince holds them back
With the slow beating of his wings.

THE EAGLE

My father crossed the Gothard range
Where waters fall...
And then along the coast towards Etruria
And by a straight route
Across the snows
Towards where Hemos and Olympus stand
And Athos casts a shadow
Towards Lemnos' caves.
Natives from the strongly perfumed forests
Of the Indus,
Came the parents.
But the grandsire
Flew across the ocean
Full of penetrating thought;
And the king's golden head was all amazed
By the mystery of the waters. Then
The stormclouds gathered red above the ship
And the animals gazed dumbly at one another
Thinking only of their food.
But the mountains stand up silently around,
Where can we wish to stay?

Friedrich Hölderlin /   70

SYBIL

The storm
             bends the branches
                          And the raven sings
Thus is the time of God a journey sure

        But thou Eternal song
And the poor pilot searches for the unknown

        Look towards the star.

FORM AND SPIRIT

All is an inscape

                    And yet separates

Thus shelters the Poet

Fool! dost thou hope from face to face
                          To see the soul

                          thou shalt go among the flames.

TO THE BELOVED (DIOTIMA)

Elysium

        There with certainty I find

        Towards you, Gods of Death

        There Diotima   Heroes

71   / Friedrich Hölderlin

I would sing of thee

But only tears

And in the night in which I walk I see extinguish thy
Clear eyes!

O spirit of the Sky.

'AM I NOT FAR FROM THEE'

Am I not far from thee

Yet I am calmed

When I was a child, she was

the sister.

Yet now at last,

Thou wanderest where art thou

Where art thou?

'– PEACEFULLY THE NECKAR'

peacefully the Neckar

And the island

but above

the crowded room.

There, there

        Neither hear nor see
           a river.
    then, then, cry out, that there may be light.

      O graces of the sky,
               and that the festival
Of the gods of Joy may fall upon that day!

GREECE

                         roads of the traveller?
For   shadows of trees
Hillsides, in the sun
Where the road leads
To (the) church.
        rains like arrows of rain
And trees sleeping standing up, and yet
At the appointed time there come the footsteps of the sun
And so, as the warm mist
Glistens above the town,
So walks the sun upon the walls
And curtains of the rain

And as the ivy hangs
So hangs the branchless rain.
But with more beauty for the traveller
Blossoms the road
     in freedom   and changes like the corn.

Through the Gothard the horse reaches
The woods of Avignon. The laurels
Murmur around Virgil's path –
And may the sun never
Seek unmanfully the tomb.
All mossy grows the rose
Among the Alps. At the town gates
The flowers begin

              / *Friedrich Hölderlin*

Like crystals in the desert of the seas.
The gardens grow near Windsor. And with pomp
From London drives the carriage of the King.
The beautiful gardens change with the seasons.
On the canal. But right beneath extends
The world of the sea, shining and smooth.

AUTUMN

Now the legends of the spirit leave the earth.
The spirit has been, and shall come again.
The legends turn towards humanity, we learn
Much about time, which passes so soon away.

Nature does not abandon the image of the past,
And so when the high days of the summer fade,
The autumn arrives on earth,
And the spirit of the seer is once more caught into the sky.

In a short time many things have changed,
The peasant, who has taken to the plough,
Sees how the year sinks to its joyous end,
In these images accomplished is the day of man.

The roundness of the earth, with rocks adorned,
Is not like that of clouds, which in the evening melt,
But is shown to us in a single golden day,
And the perfection has no plaint.

WINTER

When pale snow decorates the countryside
And shines with a bright light on the extended plain,
The summer charms us from afar, the warmth of spring
Is often felt as the hour dies away.

Splendid are all appearances, the air more light,
The forest clear; and no man comes
Into the distant streets,
And all things smiling silence makes sublime.

Spring with its shimmer of flowers hardly seems
To please mortals as much, but the bright stars
Are very clear on high, with joy we see
The distant skies which almost never change.

The rivers, the plain and all created things,
Seem more dispersed, and clearer to the sight,
The warmth of life continues and the amplitude of towns
Seems more goodly than before in their unlimited extent.

SPRING

The sun returns to joys renewed.
The day with its sun-rays, like a flower,
Nature's adornment, to the heart appears
As hymns and songs appeared when they were born.

There is a new world in the valley's depths,
Serene is the morning hour in Spring,
And the day shines from the heights, and evening life
Also descends to meditate within.

                    ★   ★   ★

The new day from the distant heights descends,
The morning from its twilight mist awakes
And laughs at men, and men bedecked and gay
Are bathed in sweetest joy.

In days to come new life would be revealed,
It seems that the great valley and the earth
Are brimmed with flowers, the signs of days of joy,
For with the Spring the plaint has died away.

SUMMER

This is the season of the year, the countryside
Of summer in its light and warmth;
The green of the splendid fields is spread
Everywhere where the foaming stream descends.

Across the mountains and the valleys marches day
With its all-powerful strength and with its rays,
And the clouds in the high spaces pass in peace
And seem like the year passing with its glorious train.

★   ★   ★

The days pass by
With the sound of gentle airs; when they exchange
The clouds against the splendour of the fields,
The end of the valley meets the mountains' dusk;

And the shadows of the forests spread around –
Look, where the distant stream flows down below,
The image of the distance is seen passing in the hours
When man has found the mysterious inner sense.

PERSPECTIVES

The open day is clear in images to man,
When the green of a distant view appears,
Before the clarity of evening towards twilight sinks
And the sounds of day by gentle echoes are prolonged.

Often the inner world is closed and full of clouds,
Man's mind perturbed and full of doubt,
But splendid Nature has rejoiced in its fine days
And doubt with its sombre questions stands far off.

★   ★   ★

When into the distance pass away
The lives of men,
There in the distance shines the vineyard season,
And present also are the empty fields of summer
And the dark image of the forest rises up.

That nature the seasons' images should multiply,
That she should stay while they slide swiftly on,
Is the ordainment of perfection; and the heights
Of the sky shine radiantly for man,
And the tree is crowned with flowers.

TINIAN

Pleasant to wander
In the sacred desert

★   ★   ★

And at the she-wolves' dugs, good spirit,
At the waters, those who wander
Through their native land
                              once wild,

Now tamed, to drink
Like the lost child found;
During spring, when foreign wings
Coming back out of the warm depths of the woods.

                    the day in solitude reposing
And about the sprouting palms
The bees reassemble
With the summer birds

★   ★   ★

/ Friedrich Hölderlin

                                    for there are flowers
Which grow not from the earth,
They grow out of themselves from the barren soil,
A reflection, it's unlucky
To gather such flowers,
Gold, already they have lost their petals
Like thoughts.

[UNTITLED]

O sure foundations of the Alps
Which   ★   ★   ★

And O tranquil gazing mountains
Where above the bush-grown slopes
The black forest sighs
And the foliage of the pines distributes
Odour, and the Neckar
                        and the Danube!

The gentle fever in the summer
Surrounds the gardens and the
Lindens of the village,
Where the aspen and the rowan
Strew the sacred grass with flowers
And   ★   ★   ★

You good towns!
Unspotted, with the enemy
Powerlessly mingled

That   ★   ★   ★
And for once goes away
And has no perception of death
But   ★   ★   ★

And the lightnings fall
In the clear light in which
Spizberg leans
And the goodly smells

And the Thills Thal, which ★ ★ ★
And Stuttgart, where I
The man of a short moment
Am to be buried, there
Where the street becomes
             the vineyard path
And once again the rumour of the town
Is heard below in the green spaces
And beneath the apple-trees.

REMEMBRANCE

The north-east wind is risen
The wind that I of all love best
Because to all seafaring men it means
A calm sea and a prosperous voyage.

Take thy departure, then, and bear my greetings to
The lovely land of the Garonne
And to the gardens of Bordeaux, where yonder far
The pathway on the abruptly rising bank
Goes on and on, where the river streams deep down
Leaves from above him bend
And gaze at him a noble pair
Of oaks, and silver poplar-trees.

I still remember it all well, still can I see
The stout trunks of the forest of elm trees
That stands above the mill
But there's a figtree in the courtyard grows
Thither on days of festival
The browncheeked countrywomen go
Over the soil as soft as silk

          / *Friedrich Hölderlin*

When March has come
When night and day are both of equal length
And when on the slow-winding banks
With its light freight of shining
Dreams the breeze goes with its swinging lullaby

Ah, hand the goblet on

With black light filled and lift
The goblet cavernous
Which shall bring us repose! O sweet
Then to sink down among the shades
Is it not good (meet)
When mortal thoughts uprise
To give one's soul up? – yet
Communion too is good, and to give speech
To the heart's thoughts, to hear discussed at length
The days of lovers and the great
Events that using them have come to pass.

But where are those I loved? Bellarmin
With his companion? Many a man
Is scared of going back right to the source.
Yes, it is the sea that is
The place where primal riches lie.
                                            They
Like painters, gather into one place
The beauties of the earth and do in nowise scorn
The wingèd war-god nor   ★   ★   ★

FRAGMENT

And in that far off distance you speak thus to me
In the eternal jubilation of thy soul.
'What is it you call happiness? And what
Is what you call misfortune?' I do hear
O Father! asked this question. But there also to my ear
Is brought the sound of waves, in which I drown, seeming to dream
Of a most precious pearl lost in the ocean's deepest bed.

THE WALK

After Friedrich Hölderlin

You beauteous forests on the slope
Painted against the wall of green,
Where I make my random way
Rewarded by the sweet respite
From every hurt my scarred heart's had
When the insight's been made dark,
For the price of such insight and of art
Must ever by suffering be paid.
Pleasing pictures of the valley,
As for example gardens, tree,
And also the foot-path that is strait.
The stream is scarcely to be seen
How fine in the joyful distance shines
For somebody the great picture
Of the land that I most willingly
Visit when weather's favourable.
The Divinity comes in friendliness
To lead us with the blue above,
And later with the clouds that have
Gathered, arched and ashy grey,
With flashing lightnings
                              and the sound
Of the ensuing thunder's growl,
With the charm of the pasture-fields,
With the beauty that springs and flows
From the primaeval Picture's source.

THE CHURCHYARD

After Friedrich Hölderlin

A silent spot made green by new-grown grass
Where man and woman lie asleep, where crosses stand
Where friends are brought in from the world outside
Where shining are the clear glass window-panes

When the lofty sky sheds down on you its light
At noon, when often springtime dwells there still,
When an etherial cloud floats grey and damp above
And softly daylight with its beauty disappears!

When silence does not wrap the high grey wall
Above which leans a tree laden with fruit;
With a dew-moistened blackness, leaves that mourn,
The fruits are none the less all finely pressed.

In the church is a dark tranquillity
And the altar also in this night is small.
Yet a few things of beauty may be found there too
But many a tree-cricket's summer song may be heard through the
    hymns

There if someone hears the pastor preach
Where the crowd of friends remains near by
Who are with the one who's died, how much personal life
And spirit, godly yet undisturbed.

TWO FREE ADAPTATIONS OF LATE HÖLDERLIN POEMS
(in honour of Charles Causley)

1   *TO ZIMMER*

I say of a man: If he is wise and good,
What more can be needful? Is there aught enough
To suffice a soul? Can any possession,
Grape of the best-ripened vine on earth,

Be thought to sustain him? And therefore the meaning
Is this. A friend is frequently the beloved one,
And art far more so. O my dear, I tell you this truth:
You contain the spirit of Dedalus and of the forests.

Friedrich Hölderlin /   82

2 SUNDAY

. . . .
Friendship and love, church and the saints, crucifix, pictures,
Altar, pulpit and music. The sermon composed for him.
The catechism after dinner is a drowsy converse
For the men and children, girls and devout women;
After which the squire, the commoner and the artist go out to the
    joyful fields,
On to the native meadow, and the young people go off in reflective
    mood.

/ *Friedrich Hölderlin*

Georges Hugnet (1906 – 74)

POEM

The chrysalis says she is the fern's perfection,
chance of being's will,
the hatchway is a grain of salt on a frigate's sail,
the doors are pieces of shadow, the drawers are at play,
the triangles are earthen,
indolence is reddish, the lama's nose is a window,
good-morning chases a fly on to the ceiling,
the walls are the halt of the ultramarine and the roof is a pump,
your face does not exist,
my love is well polished,
the sea interrogates its beaches secretly,
living is not following a mirror's movements as best one can,
the winged ant is an ear,
tears are the beggars who roll to the bottom of ponds,
a room is the bother of leaving it,
entering it is to allow oneself everything, I wish you were chilly,
desolation is a bunch of papers,
the wind is a hand, the hand a raspberry,
when the sea comes up, chance threads a needle,
the shine of your fingernails is echoed by the apples,
looking is not for much more than a pillow-case,
habit is the eye and speaking is black,
if I ask myself questions I dress in beetle,
reason is the same as fear:
the little green spot that shakes about in the red sea,
blood is a sculpture,
a book or the wherewithal to die,
the addressee of a letter is an island-shaped stain,
your hair is an ant-hill, a medlar-tree before a cheval-glass,
presence and solitude are two beans in a black room,
two beans facing one another,
to give shade one turns on the same switch
that immortalizes the last cigarette of a man condemned to death
and there you have the beheading of human justice,
sleeping is a word
and oracle a mania; egg, awakened dreamer,
neither humility nor vanity is my strong point,

the tree is a dandyism,
a tower goes down the river, Barbary fig,
you are my only pride, I am only pride before you,
the images are not sufficiently distant,
the giraffe is the year's longest eyelash,
one must renounce all commentary,
unlearn all that was learnt
and live only in the incredible
in order to live.

POEM

A mail-coach overturns in the meadow
that the ninepins were tormenting
it all adds to the uneasiness of autumn on this race-course
where flame puts Gyges' ring
and the reputedly incurable crimsons
into luxury's prison
when the chess-board ruled the situation
the chance decision
slid out of the bull's-eye
towards the orphan girl
She suggested various improvements
to the glow-worms of the waiting-room
The sound of lanterns is heard afar
transmitted by the way of suicide
She then replaces her mother's photograph
by a glass of Tokay
in which she bathes her breasts
whatever the direction of the wind may be
or whoever may be looking on
as she once saw done with silver-paper
The wardrobe opens in a twinkling of an eye
she hastens through the savage glen
The writing-expert sets out to contradict the chimes
all comparisons lead to the morrow
O little adopted girl my carven stone
valid on fountain trust
colour that smokes in hair
and never varies.

/ Georges Hugnet

Edmond Jabès (1912 – 91)

THE FAREWELL

'Every book is written in the transparency of a farewell,' he said.

'A day comes when you have to consent to stay silent, when words have no longer any need of you,' he also said.

Stay silent. Go to earth.

The wise old man says to his disciple:

'Write down, to my dictation, what my hand can no longer, so great is its weakness, consign to the page,' then closes his eyes and drops into a drowse.

From this collusive silence is born the book of the primordial night, which will later engender the book of days.

When each star is a salvaged word.

A night for death; a day for life.

Unchangeable is the altering cycle of the years.

Autumn is at the heart of the seasons.

'Dawn is not the farewell' – he had noted –; 'but every farewell is the dazzling daring of a dawn.'

Tomorrow: the guilty horizon.

And the wise man says: 'To God falls the burthen of the Whole.'

'To man, his share of the scant.'

From the *Livre de l'hospitalité*

Max Jacob (1876 – 1944)

TWO POEMS FROM LE CORNET À DÉS (The dice-box)

I.   *THE KEY*

   When the lord of Framboisy returned from war, his wife severely reproached him in church, whereupon he said: 'Madame, here is the key to my estate, I am going away for ever.' The lady let the key fall to the paved floor of the house of prayer out of delicacy. In a corner, a nun was praying because she had mislaid her own, the convent key, and no one could get in. 'Then see whether your lock and this key fit.' But the key was no longer there. It was already in the Cluny Museum: an enormous key in the shape of a tree-trunk.

II.   *THE TRUE MIRACLES*

   The good old parish-priest! after he'd left us, we saw him flying away above the lake like a bat. He was so absorbed in his thoughts that he didn't even notice the miracle. The lower part of his cassock was wet, which astonished him.

GLIMMERS IN THE DARKNESS

Juggle no more, Protagoras. Within you silence has now come.
To sing of you, O hills, what power have I?
God, thou makest the verdure and the harvest-time.
Poet, have you no sense of gratitude
To him who dictated this song to you?
A day will soon be dawning when the old countryside
Will lull with the sea both my flame and my voice,
When beneath your trees, O mountain, I shall find once more
The rhythm I am searching for and which would suit
Orpheus shedding tears for his Eurydice.

What is to me then truly worth the Axe of Victories?
What truly matter to me the Kabbalah and History?
I am tired of talking, I am tired of tales,
Of literature and of ancient monuments.

Nature! Glaucous ocean! O woods! vast stretches of heath!
You are my loves! autumn of the auburn mane!
Mossgrown apple-trees! It is of you that I would sing
If the Muse would only teach my pen to work!

But no! the fire goes out, and your wing too turns pale,
The countryside gives way! inspiration's flood withdraws.
Poet, you're nothing more, when reduced to your simple self,
Than a hick grammarian, curler of comma-tails,
And you, evil demons waging war on me,
Your task's accomplished for the man I used to be.
The pedant reappears. I am vanquished once again.

Pierre Jean Jouve (1887 – 1976)

FIVE POEMS

1. *WOMAN AND EARTH*

Was stronger than the light this heart which beat in her,
Her blood to the moon's influence more open lay
Than lifeblood shed; her night was denser and more hirsute than
The Night, and just as sparkling and as hard –
More sex than soul a star more than a sex
Temple with tresses drifting from the dome

Are sleeping now that other granite, roses overblown
That pass away and vanish in the light's pure lake –
Old weakness felt no more, all distance done away:
O lofty lofty lands and alien azure sky
Weigh down on her who now is no more known
As bosom or as spasm or as hot tears spilt in Time:
Who underneath the ground has turned right round
To face another, a more ashen sun.

2. *THE MOTHS*

There are moths shut-in below
Moths pink and black and plump
Such moths are warm with an inhuman glow
Their wings are faults of memory
These creatures have the accent of two faces marked by fate
When they are hanging strictly folded-up below.

When the moths of the flesh below are called
Up from the shadows where they wait
They rise up pink and plump
They rise up but they flap
They flap but soon are swollen tight
With odour, blindness, nudity and weight.

3. BROW

The sun's come back upon the window-panes
The birds make song
And Hope invades the window-panes
Of golden-fired insurgent Morn.
Revolutions make dank mansions shake
While in the gracious light the Heroes march
And down across the blue roofs the bared heads
Of families of remorseless tyrants fall –

When Man bound to his evil fate
Is dead
Struck down by the myriad blows that he so well deserved
Behold his brow take form in the calm blue on high!

4. NADA

The most beautiful most naked and most tragic splendours
The oppositions between suns and darknesses
In night's forever black protective space
The deepest ecstasy in unknown arms

All things that are no more
And yet are born in agony at dawn
See thee and lift thee up ineffable uproar
Innumerable flaming fireless sex of stars

Love's flame too flaming and too crucified
Upon the intimate blackness of our eyes
Desert of love
Organ of God.

5. *THE TWO WITNESSES*

Have pity, O harsh Lamb upon these last two
Witnesses who shall in scarlet cloak be slain and have no tomb
And take O Liberty into thy charge their red remains
For these are the two holy candle-bearers of the Lord
For they have been given power to shut the sky
For their mouths' fire has quite consumed the unjust man
For they have turned the waters into blood
But at last the Beast of the abyss
Has been sent power to deliver them
Has made war and has killed them and all their deeds has undone.

THE DESIRES OF THE FLESH
ARE A DESIRE FOR DEATH

The desires of the flesh are a desire for death
And the desire for flight is earthly, of the earth
The love of gold is the great cities' excrement
Desires of youth are all a greed for graves

As hard some hungers are as a woman's nakedness
I make love on the daily bed I lie in pain
Drowsy with light the pearls of morn lie strewn
Along death's green-marged shore

O, it was not in vain that Christ's sweet saints
Did with the devil wage long bitter war
Nor is it all in vain that Christ's and the devil's breasts
Are made to seem one and the same in this deep night

O take account but of the tears' weight, not
For their own sake, but for the voids they leave behind
And sliding in black vertigo down the sheer sides of this
Obliterated world: draw nigh, draw nigh unto the One.

/ Pierre Jean Jouve

TRANSPIERCE ME LORD WITH MY OWN GRIEF

Transpierce me Lord with my own grief
Give work to the machinery of my tears
Remove from me my last repose
And drive me from my knowledge, Pitiless One

Soul! filled with music O surround
My ugliness unceasingly like an erotic shade
Giving direction to my pains

O pensive Soul of God
Silent when I cried out in hunger or joy
Most beautiful (and to be dealer to me of my death)

Suave eucharist
To be devoured by my mouth's bloodless lips
Thou knowest how in blindness I pray unto thee
O wounded side death can no more corrupt

The deeper sin, the more truthful the light
And higher like a flag on high
Torn but resplendent from its black
Worn backward-leaning flagstaff knowledge flies

A LONE WOMAN ASLEEP

When there came days sunk deep in damp your beauty seemed
    increased
And ever warmer grew your glow when rain fell in despair
And when days came that were like deserts you
Grew moister than the trees in the aquarium of time
And when the ugly anger of the world raged in our hearts
And sadness lisped exhausted through the leaves
You became as sweet as death
Sweet as teeth in the ivory skull-box of the dead
And pure as the skein of blood
Your laughter made to trickle down from your soul's parted lips

When there come days deep-sunk and damp the world grows still
    more dark
When days like deserts come, the heart is drenched with tears.

FROM *NUL N'EN ÉTAIT TÉMOIN*

Austere nudity of the erotic Helen
Thou my prayer in stone and wind
Smile and insult through the rending veil
Woman too greatly beautiful beyond the passing years
Mourning memory green grass.

(Kyrie)

INSULA MONTI MAJORIS

How tender were the rocks upon the marsh
How hard the rocks were in the rock

How the birds climbed in the eternal sky
How the winds swung to and fro
The summer earth's black essences

How violently those suns beat down upon the plague
How frightened were those hearts
To be deprived of woman's sex
How deeply slept the shadows in the shadow of the stones

How holy was the terror of the day
Around the sounding stone
Their stony modulation was without fault
They sang

/ Pierre Jean Jouve

How sepulchral and giant was their soul
That God had pierced with a wound greater than the soul!
How far had they gone out from woman's womb
And how the odour became sweet out of their tombs!

How black were those white men against the fine day's light
Sleeping yet never asleep
For the Master was in agony always
Until the end of time beneath the glowing sky.

THE RESURRECTION OF THE DEAD

Man's blood, and hope, and human memory
From the black-tinged ingredients of space
That Daniel's lion-den beneath the smouldering eye
The blue hole of the heavenly throne

The great skies have been raised up like high walls
The black of cracks is outlined by the bluish sheen of steel
The millions of the judgment called, like planets all too pale
With memories of underneath the earth, go flying past

And the harlot seated high upon the waters, and
Downfallen, the great death poured from the cups
And I have seen what blows the heavenly host endures
And the white giant who has a dagger in his mouth

I've seen the only liberty there is vanquished by death
Beneath the swaddling-linen of the sky
Bathed in the black blood of the cups and wounds
When the great harlot of the waters had burst into flame

I was a man; O now illumine my remains!
And grant me pardon if I lived but for a Beast
And if I was voluptuously in love with lovely Death,
I was the poet: O illumine the whole

And if thou wast not God I will establish still
On Nothing over Nothingness the soul's supremacy,
For God not of the dead but of the living is the God
And no more can they die, the risen dead.

GRAVIDA

The rocky path is sown with sombre cries
Archangels keeping guard over the gorges' weight
The naked stones beneath the twilight waves
Are emerald green with foam and blood.

How beautiful! in illustration the sad mountainside
Sings of the death but not of the warm sex of night
Which trembles as it passes endlessly away
Towards that awesome place where I have always longed to live.

There, wall and bitter frontier, smell of wood,
Of tears and manure
And the touching son trembles once more to see
How hard is what was tender when he saw it in the womb.

WHEN GLORY'S SPRING RETURNS

The sun sheds its incandescence on the new-sprung shoots,
A sun no eyes ever beheld, there were none pure enough –
Sun rearisen after the combustion of long death.
The Spring of ancient glories is all crystal and fresh air
And the works of the great masters – Dante, Virgil – now appear
As sacred garments that adorn the naked outward form
In which they walk abroad. One may perceive
As with miraculous candour the child Baudelaire shewed forth
And Delacroix and Courbet from their tents of light emerged
To reassume eternally their golden fleece of dream.
From high savannahs of the air Rimbaud smiles down at last.

/ Pierre Jean Jouve

FROM *SUEUR DE SANG* (1933)

I
I not in vain beheld that bitter sex. The woman's back
In its appearance gleaming. Silence of the birds
On that day now among mild shades sunk dated down.

Miracle of the voice, O if my work endure,
Did you then rise from circumstances desert–like as these,
That did such evil to the soul, of one so pure?

II
The sky is intimately hid in cloudy sky
The clouds are in the water and the water in the house
The house within the heart, the latter in
Despair, but such despair within the heart
The heart inside the house, the house in space,
Space stricken with human sickness beneath the sky –

The angel of destruction sets to work; and I rejoice.

FROM *LANGUE*

I
During the moulting season of the formless final world
The conquerors held out still: alone and without horses either of
    plaster or of gold
And without money (lost in the sands and in the circuses, and on all
    fronts)
Without even a moist lance's oriflamme. And then what thrusts
    of troops that never moved!
Pure conquerors of ancient time – and all cathedrals in their train –
They awaited with their passion in the swarming towns of dwarfs
An extraordinary onslaught of empty emotion and explosiveness
Which might enable all to be recovered by the vitals that were losing
    all their blood.

II

Ah! the poet writes only for the heavens' empty space
Pure blue that winter can no longer see! he writes in conjuration of
the silence of the snows
Of the stifling of fallacious festal days! and in the lack and in the
lacklustre it reveals, each line he writes is just as though he were
not there (and his slim figure, dressed as a matador, is just as
though he were not there),
And in his solitude devoted to that admirable, secret conjuration,
behold him pleading his peculiar loves
When none would undertake to risk love's courage in his stead:

Then on the fabled winds' black shore, over the seaweeds' slumber,
under nearly weightless whirling swells of fog,
He seals the word up in the bottle of green glass,
Bells of despair and horrible seawrack!
He launches on the highest wave a bottle without action, force or
aim, yet which one day
The waves will wash up to love's level, beyond beauty, beyond
glory, beyond day.

III

Clear light of day! flow once more through the furrow you have
worn upon the mortal avenues,
Gleam on the capitals and globes of stone, waken the sacred snakes,
All men's activities! And mortal thought of mine pursue once more
Your way towards hope's narrow zone, with great deliberate works
in view:
Both works and death before my eyes stand like glad monuments
devoured by the sky's plants,
Pure ruin well contented to be filled with its vast future and its natural
love.

/ Pierre Jean Jouve

FREEDOM OR DEATH

I see it once again, in rather a sombre, a windless corner, tight-stretched and unwrinkled by any fold. The stuff it was made of was softest silk, which seemed to make a profound, suave, unsounding music; consisting of three cruelly torn pieces, each seeming enlarged by the (two) others.

That which first made my *heart stand still* was the crimson piece; not crimson though, no, rose-red, as of a rose with crushed and dried up petals; yet rose-blossom red, did I say? not so; but in a sort of anguish verging on lilac, of a graver tone, that exquisite tone that the assassinated victim's blood has acquired at last, the blood of Marat.

IN HELEN'S LAND

After Pierre Jean Jouve

Like some deposit dropped from a mystic sky
Yonder intones an organ hewn of rock: which leaning, pores
Over the rain's grey shadow as though over its own thought;
But what is in its heart? There Helen lies.

This is the shattered rock of Helen's majesty and state
Which rules over that uterine deep land
Wherein her milkwhite flesh had life; and where
She met her death, in splendour, sick with love, adorned with
    flowers,

Where naked forests trembled at her breath.

EVENING PRAYER

After Pierre Jean Jouve

O Thou to all eternity God of my love,
My prayer beholds Thee in this silence dense and dark
Whereunto I after yet one more day am come:
Sacred the dark, wretched the ragged wound,
Wound wedded to the darkness and with peace welded as one.
O God, Thou art substantial made through Thy rebirth by night,
Out of Thy absence, from that grievous wound no less;
Thou art as the pure void and all else emptiness is blind,
Thou art the lamb of jet-black fleece whereon clear may the brand
Of death be read, though letterless; and now allow the wound
To close, as closely the soft curtains to be drawn that shelter hope.

FROM *GÉNIE*

Helen's sweet laughter pierces the panes to reach
The solid wall upon the heights; and the cold lakes
Weep joyful tears for a hundred acts of love and shame
Of transport and desire over those most strange plants
Sent here in memory of her, at the pure hour
When warming 'neath the sensual velvet of another sky
Aurora combing her gold hair beckoning her towards death.

TO HIMSELF

Write now only for the sky
Write for the curved arc of the sky
And to no black letter of lead
Resort to wrap thy writing in
Write for the odour and the breath
Write for the sheet of silver leaf
Let no unlovely human face

Have glimpse or knowledge or rumour thereof
Write for the god and for the fire
Write for the sake of a beloved place
And may nothing to do with man intrude.

PIETÀ

Maternal shadow, closely to you do you hold
His dying body on the brink of madness.
Hold him to you close. To see him still means ah!
                    What rending shreds
Of sacred horror binding your softness round with love
O memory
Mindful how starkly you were destitute
And mindful of how his body out of yours,
                    that body's soul,
Once was torn forth when black fires
                    split across your brow.

                                        (Fragment)

[UNTITLED]

Here the sky, the vast sky is full of gusts of wind and rock
O harden the sky blue rock and make the rock's air quiver
How steely sounds the singing of the antique violin's strings
How gentle feels the stroking of the genius's green heart

How precious is the rock with its mounds of unburnt ash
How pure, how out of season is the great mass of gold!
How chilly feels the fervour slipping into the lips below
Of the inviolable hymen of the day.

                    Translated by David Gascoyne and Roger Scott

Valery Larbaud (1881 – 1957)

LONDON

Having fallen in love with eyes in Burlington Arcade,
I walk back in a leisurely way down Piccadilly.
Oh, breaths of Spring mingling with smells of urine
Between the railings of Green Park and the taxi-rank,
How poignant I find you!
Then, I follow Rotten Row, towards calmer Kensington,
Less poetic, less under the spell
Of those colours, those smells and of London's roar.
(O Johnson, I understand your heart, learned Doctor,
Heart so resounding with the noise of the great city:
Fleet Street's horizon was sufficient to your eyes.)

O green and blue gardens, white mists, mauve veils!
Barring the dull platinum water of the pool
Sleeping beneath the intangible gauze of a rich fog,
The long wake left by a rust-plumaged sea-bird . . .

There's the Thames, that Madame d'Aulnoy
Deemed 'one of the fairest waterways in the world'.
Its historic figures sailed on it, in Summer,
As evening fell, disturbing the white reflection
Of the first stars;
And the barges, hung with silk, laden with princes
And ladies reclining on square embroidered cushions,
And Buckingham and the Queen's noblewomen,
Moved slowly forward, like a dream, over the water,
Or as my heart would once long let itself be rocked
By the fine rhythms of Albert Samain's regal lines.
The shining street where all can admire their own
        reflections;
The many-coloured bus, the black cab, the girl in pink
And even a certain amount of sunset, one might say . . .
The washed roofs, the square all bluish and smoking . . .
The soiled copper clouds slowly climbing upwards . . .
Lull and humid lukewarmness, and tobacco's honey smell;
The gilding of this book

Becomes clearer every moment: the sun trying to break through no
　　doubt.
(Too late, the night will inevitably take it away.)
And here's the barrel-organ bursting into sound now the downpour's
　　gone.

From *Les Poésies de A.O. Barnebooth* (1913)

WESTON-SUPER-MARE: NOON

The rain will fall the whole day long
Upon the terraces which rise
Between the ever-moving sky
And the solemn regions where
The White Sun's Empire wields its sway.

The Unknown-Mountain veils itself,
And the guardians of the tidal mouth,
That stranded pair of elephants,
Plunge into the immeasurable mist
And set off for the silver isle.

But in the garden sad and blue
Brooding upon this gloomy noon,
Where the creased nasturtium blooms
Collapse and mingle, in a crowd,
Their yellow-orange and red array;
After a moment one comes across,
Just when I thought I was most alone,
Sheltered beneath the porch the nest
Whence clusters of clear and quiet eyes
Are watching the garden while it steams.

Oh! how the rain makes them well-behaved,
And how controlled their silence is!
And how attentive are they now
To these eye-whites all astir
In the black box and laurel trees!

Is that Crazy Maisie there,
And Gladys laughing all the time;
Violette with knees forever grazed
And Gwenny who always has to throw
Her shuttle-cock over the wall?

From *Les Poésies de A.O. Barnebooth* (1913)

Giacomo Leopardi *(1798 – 1837)*

AN IMITATION OF LEOPARDI'S IMITATION CANTO *(XXV)*

Far from your bough
Poor fragile leaf,
Whither away? – From the beech
Which gave me birth the wind has wrested me;
Since when, in ever-whirling flight
From the woods towards the plain
It sweeps me off, and from the dale up to the hills.
Along with it, wayfarer
I pass on without rest, knowing nought else.
I go whither all things hie,
Whither nature decrees
The rose-leaf must go,
And the laurel likewise.

After La Feuille of Antoine-Vincent Arnault (1768-1834)

A SE STESSO: TO HIMSELF *AFTER CANTO XXVIII*

Now may you lie still forever,
My wornout heart. The utmost illusion
I once deemed eternal has perished. Deceased. Well I know
That of all those once cherished illusions
Not only hope but desire is now quenched.
Lie still forever. You have been throbbing
Long enough. Nothing merits your ardour, this earth
Is not worth sobbing for. Bitterness, tedium:
Nought else is our life; the world is a mire.
From henceforward be mute. Give up hope
The last time. Fate grants to our kind
The right only to die. Henceforth hold in contempt
Not yourself only, but Nature, the arrogant power
That consigns us in secret to ruin,
And the everlasting emptiness of All.

Stéphane Mallarmé (1842 – 98)

SUMMER SADNESS

after Mallarmé

The sun, O sleeping wrestler, on the sand
Makes warm a languid bath in your hair's gold,
Mingles with tears a loving-cup might hold
The incense burning on your cheek unkind.

This blazing white and never changing calm
Has made my timid kisses, saddened, cry:
'Never shall we a lonely mummy lie
Beneath the antique desert and the happy palm!'

And yet your tresses are a tepid stream
In which our soul might drown unshuddering
And find that void of which you only dream.

I'd taste the paint which from your lids runs down
To see if it could give the heart you wring
The hard insentience of sky or stone.

Loys Masson (1915 – 69)

POEM OF THE FORMS OF GRACE

When you lay your hands in the Lord's hands as night falls on the
    sleeping fields
O my comrades weave me a paradise with your free hands!
I've lived nailed to freedom in a time when tyrants nailed it to the cross
their breast heaved like the flank of hills when lightning heralds
    thunder
massacres stuck like a madrepore of blood to their men's skin
Remember me: I have been sower and soldier
Under the peak of scaffolds I have sown the rape-seed of the oil of
    wrestlers
of fully-booked seasons when armed supporter-bands were on watch
The flax of your hope has ripened under my wrists
Silently revolt counted its cartridges in my loins
Spring came to rub its young shoots against my legs

Remember me when you break bread during the nights of vigil
Remember me when angels at the wine-press pray over your crushed
    grapes
Under the tyranny high as Babel I've fought like one who will fight
    no more, my brothers
I've bled like one who will no longer bleed, dress my wounds with
    insects and green leaves
Make the sparrow come and perch on my shoulders that they've
    laden with chains
the mole under my knees dig his summer mole-hills
O my comrades I cry towards you from the depths of the loam of fire
I hear your footsteps approach in the footsteps of my God
high up above, where the ice-cold eyes of the executioners cannot
    reach
On your prairies I will live again with outstretched arms, like two
    silos visited by sky-birds;
From my earthy hands in the morning the swallow will take flight
At the sound of the angelus shadow will girdle my sides with a lace
    of seeds
Mary will be that bright star kissing the brow of the branches
– My axe will bear iris-flowers on its edge

When Christ of the olive-trees shall be Christ of the wheat-ears, the
    mills grinding at his feet
gentle mares betrothed to his crucified-one's thorns
When man on man's shoulder shall have his field and his house
My brothers I will return.
The peaceable wind will crown me with rye and hops
Tranquil my wife will shine on the edge of the woods
in the assumption of Freedom.

THE PASTOR ESSENDEAN, INSTEAD OF A CHRISTMAS PRESENT, READS FROM A GREEN BIBLE BOUND IN BISHOP'S SKIN

In the beginning, there was nothing; and nothing smelt of lemon and myrrh and male lavender.

Then around nothing, the night encoiled itself: the night bit its tail and the infinite was created.

Then there were twelve stars of the glory of God and around each of these stars twelve others; and twelve stars of the glory of Satan; and twelve worms for the tombs of the twelve first angels.

Then there were the mauve-collared diseases: the Plague, Smallpox, Work, and the rest. There was a pox of the sky under the name of clouds, a plague of the night which was called day. And space was in labour with the earth for seven years.

The earth was born, the dawn was born dancing on one foot. There was the first rain and the seasons, mirroring themselves in a lake, could compose faces for themselves.

Satan invented weight and beneath it he put the earthly animals. Then to put a check to him God invented the feather, and beneath it he put songs under the appellation of birds. In collaboration, God and Satan made man.

Trees, trunks and branches, sprang from the slime. The Tree of Science was electric and the forbidden fruit the first arc-lamp.

Original sin was committed one Sunday...

O.V. de L. Milosz (1877 – 1939)

H*

The garden descends towards the sea. Poor garden, garden without
    flowers, blind
Garden. On her bench, an old woman clad
In glossy mourning, yellowed with the memento and the portrait,
Watches the vessels of time departing. The nettles, in the great
    emptiness

Of two-o'clock, hairy and black with thirst, keep watch.
As though from the depths of the heart of the most lost of days, the
    bird
Of the dull district chirps in the bush of slag.
The peace is the same as the terrible stillness of men devoid of love.
    And I,

I too am there, for this is my shadow; and in the sad and vile
Heat she has let her empty head fall back upon
The bosom of the light; but I,
Body and soul, myself am like the rope

About to break. What is it then that's throbbing so in me.
But what is it that's throbbing so, groaning I know not where
In me, like the rope about the capstan
Of sailing-vessels ready to depart? Too wise

Mother, eternity, ah! let me live my day!
And no longer call me Lemuel†; because down there
In a sunlight night, the lazy girls
Hail the islands of their singing and veiled youth! The sweet

---

*   H (the middle letter of the Hebrew alphabet) was added to the name of Abram
    (Abraham) and Sara (Sarah) after initiation.

†   Proverbs xxxi.

And heavy mourning murmur of the wasps of noon
Floats low above the wine and there is a kind of craziness
About the look of dew upon the hills of my beloved
Shady ones. In the religious gloom the brambles

Have seized hold of the girl's hair of sleep. Yellow in the shade
The water difficultly breathes beneath the heavy, low forget-me-not
    blue sky.
That other suffers too, bearing like the king
Of the world, a wounded side; and from his scarred-tree wound

There flows the purest stream ever to quench the thirsty heart.
And there is the crystal bird that sweetly trills
In the old somnambulistic jasmine-tree of childhood.
I will enter in there gently raising the rainbow

And I will go straight to the tree where the eternal bride
Awaits amidst the mists of the native land. And in the fires of time
    there will appear
The sudden archipelagoes, the sonorous hulks –
Peace, peace. All that is no more. All that is no longer here, my son
    Lemuel.

The voices you hear no longer come from things.
That which has long lived in the dark in you
Calls you from the garden on the mountain! From the kingdom
Of the other sun! And here, it is the disillusioned fortieth
Year, Lemuel.
The poor long time.
A water warm and grey.
A garden burnt.

UNFINISHED SYMPHONY

I

You scarcely knew me down there, under the sun of chastisement
That unites men's shadows, never their souls,
On the earth where the hearts of benumbed men
Travel alone through the darks and terrors, without knowing their
    destined land.

It was long ago – listen, bitter love of the other world –
It was far, far away – hearken to me, sister of this present world –
In the North of our birth, where a scent from the primal past ascends
From the large water-lilies of the lakes, a fume of fabulous engulfed
    orchards.

Far from our archipelagoes of ruins, lianas and harps,
Far from our fortunate mountains.
– There was a lamp and a sound of hatchets in the haze
I remember,

And I was alone in the house you never knew,
The house of childhood, the dumb, dark house,
Deep in the leafy parks wherein the chill bird of morning
Softly sang for the love of the long-since dead, in the sombre dew.

It was there, in those vast drowsily-windowed rooms
That the ancestor of our family line once lived,
And it was there that my father, his long journeys done,
Went back to die.

I was alone and, I remember,
It was the season when the wind of our native lands
Bears with it a breath of wolves, sedge and rotting flax
And sings old child-snatcher's lays in the ruins of the night.

II

The last evening had come and with it fever,
Sleeplessness and fear. And I could not recall my name.
The guard had no doubt gone to the priest's house
For the lantern no longer stood on the footstool.

O.V: de L. Milosz /   110

All our old servants were dead; their children
Had emigrated; I was a stranger
In the slanting house
Of my childhood.

The smell of that silence was just like that of corn
Found in a tomb; and no doubt you know
That moss of the mute places, sister of the buried
And coloured like a full moon low over Memphis.

For a long while I had travelled the world with my restless
Brother; and had lain awake with anguish
In all the inns of this world. Now, there I was,
Already white-headed like brother cloud. And there was nobody left.

A footstep's echo, the old mouse's scuttering would have been sweet
    to me,
For what was eating my heart out made no sound.
I was like the garret's lamp at daybreak,
Like the portrait in the album of the prostitute.

Family and friends were dead. You, my sister, you were further
Away than the halo with which in bright January
The snow's mother crowns herself. And you scarcely knew me.
When you spoke, you trembled to hear the voice of my heart,

But you had met me only one single time,
In the strange light of the gaudy lamps
Among the night flowers, and there were gilded courtiers there
And I bade farewell only to your reflection in the mirror.

Solitude was awaiting me with the echo
In the sombre gallery. A child was there
With a lantern and the key
To a graveyard. The winter of the streets

Breathed a wretched odour into my face.
I believed myself followed by my weeping youth;
But beneath the lamp with Hyperion on her knees
Old age was seated; and she did not raise her head.

III
Hearken to me, my earthly sister. It was the old blue room
Of the house of my childhood.
There was I born.
It was also there

That long ago I beheld, at the festal eve gathering,
My first Christmas tree, that dead tree turned into an angel
Emerged from the deep, harsh forest,
Emerged all lit up from the ancient depths

Of the frozen forest and proceeding all by itself,
King of the snowy swamps, with its repentant and sanctified
Will-o'-the-wisps, in the beautiful silent and white countryside:
And behold the refulgent windows of the house of the well-behaved
    child.

Such olden, far-off days! so beautiful, so pure! it was the same
Room, but forever cold, but dumb and grey.
It seemed to have lost all recollection
Of the hearth and the cricket of long-ago evenings.

There were no relatives, friends or servants there any more!
There were only old age, silence and the lamp.
Old age lulled my heart as a maddened mother would a dead child,
Silence no longer loved me. The lamp went out.

But under the weight of the Mountain of darkness
I felt that Love was rising like an inner sun
Over the olden lands of memory and that I was flying
Far, far away, as I used to once in my sleeper's travels.

IV
– 'This is the third day.' – And I suddenly shivered, for the voice
Came from my heart. It was the voice of my life.
– 'This is the third day.' – And I slept no more but knew that the time
Had come for the morning prayer. But I was tired

And I thought of the things I should see once more; for there
Was the alluring archipelago and the isle of the Centre,
The misty, the pure, that vanished long ago
With the coral tomb of my youth

And fell half-asleep at the feet of the lava cyclops. And before me
On the hill, there was the ornamental fountain with
The lianas of Eden and the velvets of decay
On the steps worn by the moon's feet, and there, on the right,

In the glorious glade in the midst of the grove
The ruins coloured like the sun! and there, not a single secret
Passage! for in this desert solitude I have strayed
With speechless love, beneath midnight cloud. I know

Where to find the darkest mulberries; the tall grass
In which the stricken statue has hidden its face
Is my friend and the lizards have long known
That I am a messenger of peace, that it never thunders

In the cloud of my shadow. Everything here loves me
For everything has seen me suffer. – 'This is the third day.
Arise, I am thy sleeper of Memphis,
Thy death in the land of death, thy life in the land of life.

The most wise, the well-deserved . . . '

CANTICLE OF SPRING

Spring has returned from its distant rovings,
It brings us the heart's peace.
Raise yourself, dear head! Look, lovely countenance!
The mountain is an isle in the midst of the mists: it has recovered its
    cheerful colour.
O youth! O viburnum of the leaning house!
O season of the prodigal wasp!
The foolish virgin of Summer
Sings in the heat.

/ O.V. de L. Milosz

All is security, rapture and rest.
How beauteous the world is, beloved, how beauteous is the world!
A pensive and pure cloud has arrived from an overcast kingdom.
An amorous hush has enveloped the gold of noon.
The slumbrous nettle weighs down its ripe head
Beneath its beautiful crown of Judaea's queen.
Can you hear? Here comes the shower.
It is coming . . . it's fallen.
Love's whole kingdom emits the scent of the water's flower.
The young bee,
Daughter of the sun,
Is reconnoitering the mystery of the orchard;
I can hear the flocks bleating;
Echo replies to the shepherd.
How beauteous the world is, beloved, how beauteous is the world!
We will follow the bagpipe's tune into the forsaken place.
Yonder, in the cloud's shadow, at the foot of the tower,
The rosemary recommends sleep; and no beauty exceeds
That of the ewe's day-coloured child.
The tender moment sends us signs from the clouded hill.
Arise, proud love, lean on my shoulder;
I will spread aside the willow's tresses,
We will look down into the valley.
The flower bends, the tree shivers: they are drunk with scent.
Already, already the wheat
Is growing in silence, as in the dreams of sleepers.
Powerful love, my consummate sister,
Let us run towards where the gardens' concealed bird calls us.
Come, cruel heart,
Come, sweet countenance;
The infant-cheeked breeze is breathing on
The jasmine cloud.
The fine-footed dove comes to drink at the fountain;
How white she appears to herself in the new water!
What is she saying? where is she?
You could say she is singing in my reborn heart.
There she is now in the distance . . .
How beauteous the world is, beloved, how beauteous is the world!
The woman of the ruins calls me from the high window:
See how her tresses of wild flowers and wind
Are spread across the collapsing culvert
And I hear the sound of the streaked bumble-bee.

Old bell-ringer of innocent days.
The time, wild head, has come for us
To adorn ourselves with the berries that breathe in the shade.
The oriole sings in the most secret alley.
O sister of my thought! what is this mystery, then?
Enlighten me, awaken me, for these are things seen in a dream.
Oh! without a doubt I am sleeping.
How beauteous is life! no more falsehood, no more remorse
And from the earth rise flowers
Which are like the pardon of the dead.
O month of love, O traveller, O day of joy!
Be our guest; stay here;
You will take rest under our roof.
Your serious schemes will drowse when the winged alley murmurs.
We will feed you with bread, honey and milk.
Do not flee.
What do you have to do down there?
Aren't you at ease here?
We will shelter you from cares.
There is a beautiful secret room
In our house of rest.
There, the green shades enter through a window that opens
Onto a garden of rapture, solitude and water.
It listens . . . it lingers . . .
How beauteous the world is, beloved, how beauteous is the world!

THE BRIDGE

The dead leaves are falling in the dormant air.
Behold, my heart, how autumn has affected your dear isle:
How pale it looks!
An orphan with how tranquil a heart!
The bells are tolling, tolling at Saint-Louis-en-l'Isle
For the dead fuchsia of the barge-skipper's wife.

/ O.V. de L. Milosz

With bowed heads, two very humble old hacks are sleepily taking
    their last dip.
A big black dog is barking threats from afar.
On the bridge-stand only myself and my child:
Faded dress, weak shoulders, white face,
A bunch of flowers in her hands.
O my child! The time ahead!
For them! For us! O my child!
The time ahead!

PSALM OF THE MORNING STAR

The torrents of flocks   pour down towards
the sheepfolds   shade covers An-Dor and
Pau of the land of Esau   covers Matred Toled Beith
Aram   and all Sparad of Judea   Starred
memory   Israel's night of the soul   space
projected by lambs' eyes   Down under Artizarra
is already shining   on the brow of our Mother Iberia
      her   Schourien-Ieschouroun   withdraws
hiding his face   beneath the sackcloth of the fog
      Selah   Enough of your bleating at the sky
salted with white specks   let us go now my wall-lickers
      to the salt of the wall of accustomed tears   on the
hyssop pathway   between the bitter hedgerows   pass
lambs of the Spring beneath the shepherd's crook   of iron
      White nineteen black forty   and
thou forty-fourth   numbers traced by a
herdsman's hand   formed like little sticks   on some
wall of Bethlehem   they are more numerous than are
you up there   goat-kids of the Living One
      of the betrothed sister of the new canticle
Selah   The hand   of the cedars of
benediction   is still as slow   upon our heads
arisen from the depths of the ages   in the language of
the Western sea   in vain does Naphschi try to
intercept   a single new word   the same
heart as in the time of the fathers   beats in wood

stone and water   of all that returns there is
nothing new   all those things were sleeping
in closed books   the books have opened themselves
beneath my hand   pass my beauties Judith
pass   good girls   under the iron
crook   Kimah Ksil and you the Mazaroths
and you the other skies   nameless innumerable
suspended aloft so high   in the great
hazes of God   holy old men   cast down
towards the earth   your gazes of lost and
fractured flint   Aieleth-hascahar the shepherdess
     comes down towards Guinath Agoz   the light's
jug of milk on her shoulder   she calls to the child Olel
     guardian of the lions' pasture   caressed in
his sleep by vipers   Selah   Here things
are what they are   the eyelashes'   steam
     fires of rain at the roof-edge   in the
sower's sack handful of stars   and thy wheels
                         entering one into the other

     Iehezkeel the terrible spirals   behold how here
things are what they are   deep profoundly deep
is That   he who bows down low
will be bowed down to

From *Poésies*, Vol. II

/ O.V. de L. Milosz

Benjamin Péret (1899 – 1959)

THAT'S NO GOOD

O little dogs little dogs
Swim in the ink
in the ink that is extracted from the hair of big dogs
with stamping clogs
with chucked oranges
like an enraged cow
slowly petrifying under the eyes
of a tobacconist
It will suit you to wear neck-ties
which will perhaps be out of the running
the slip-shod slippers will drag along at the corners of streets
leading to wastelands
as a legion of honour leads to the drain
The wind will have an attack of apoplexy
and the stones will throw themselves of their own accord
at skulls ravaged by winter and its floods
to murmur afterwards The Tower beware
of the spiced bread that goes rotten by degrees
Beware of what
of the little flowers of the fields
or of the toes that shake with a great laugh
the laugh of a melon that opens
to let a dozen butterflies fly out.

THE STAIRCASE WITH A HUNDRED STEPS

The blue eagle and the demon of the steppes
in the last cab in Berlin
Legitimate defence
of lost souls
the red mill at the beggars' school
awaits the poor student
With the housemaid Know huntsmen how to hunt

on pay–day
Know huntsmen how to hunt
as papa speculates
with the smile
By the dagger the dagger the dagger
the tiger of the seas dreams of happiness
Avenged
The vestal·virgin of the Ganges cries out Vanity
when the flesh succumbs
Stop look and listen
the famous turkey spends a day of pleasure
turning round in an enchanted circle
with the pluck of a lion
M'sieur the major
My Paris
my uncle from America
my heart and my legs
slaves of beauty
admire the conquests of Nora
while someone asks for a typewriter
for the black pirate
It is not possible
that a woman dressed as the MERRY WIDOW
could become the wind's prey
because the millionairess Madame Sans-Gene
leads a wild existence
in another's skin
Her son was right
Patrol-leader 129 who wears an Italian straw-hat
and is the ace of jockeys
is abandoning a little adventuress
for a woman
It is the April-Moon which chases the buffalo
to Notre-Dame of Paris
Oh what a bore the indomitable man
with clear eyes
wishes to judge him by the law of the desert
but the lovers with children's souls have gone away
Ah what a lovely voyage

/ Benjamin Péret

AND SO ON

A kick in the pants once more
and the empty sardine-tin thinks itself holy
A kick with the heel on the jaw
and it is a divinity
which swims in pure honey
not caring about protozoons
sea-horses
or heavenly pebbles that flutter from eye to eye
and carry reason
with a little sauce and some broken teeth
into the society of cabbage-stumps
who no longer know what to do with their heads
since thick waters stifle in furs.

HONEST FOLK

The quarrel between the boiled chicken and the ventriloquist
had for us the meaning of a cloud of dust
which passed above the city
like the blowing of a trumpet
It blew so loudly that its bowler-hat was trembling
and its beard stood up on end
to bite off its nose
It blew so loudly
that its nose cracked open like a nut
and the nut spat out
into the far distance
a little cow-shed
wherein the youngest calf
was selling its mother's milk
in sausage-skin flasks
that its father had vulcanized.

SLAPPED FACE

Ah how thin the bones are when it rains
when the nurseries of Grecian noses
resound with the strident crying of red eggs
which sometimes weep beefsteak tears
perfumed like a beast of burden
when apples call for justice
and eyeglasses put out the eyes of the ministers
of the third republic
in which princes hide like chipped pots
in the recesses of wardrobes
with the new-born babies of the housemaid
who doesn't want to get the sack

Ah how fat the bones are
when the lamps of felt
yawn like broad-beans
when navels get their beards cut
and their hair
at the district barber's
who has never seen poodles
so well trained to swallow sugar
like blind-men at the corner of a quay
bicycles in a graveyard
or musicians in a drain

AT THE END OF THE WORLD

When the flaming coals flee away like frightened lions at the bottom
        of the mine
the white-wine birds
drag themselves like postage-stamps on to the letters sent back from
        abroad
and the rickety staircases
stupid as sauces whose pickled cabbage has already been eaten
wait for the break of day
and for the apples to be ripe

/ Benjamin Péret

before calling to the coach-horse
who plays hide-and-seek with his coach
and will destroy it
before the big toes of house-keepers turn into railway-lines

A BUNCH OF CARROTS

Blood blood blood of the flying codfish
May it fall back on to the toes of the wise man
may it conceal the cascades
like ghosts
and may the blood the blood of the freshly-caught codfish
drown the scraggy cows
which will be tyres and burst
at the first mosquito-bite
And their chines shall be ploughed
so scientifically
that the peasants will twist their thumbs
like shells
which will burst in the blood the blood of the flying codfish
and scatter them on every side
like a ruffled mop

FLANDERS BRIDGE

Prussian blue
The soap slides away down the banisters
and the shells of bitter almonds
ask for the white wine
which plays hide-and-seek
with the tails of the pigs
who are to be met with any day
in the corridors of hotels
They have flags and navels

and brains of brown ale
with duck hats
which wait for the snow to melt
before crying Have you seen the bride
who smells of garlic like an old cow
because the pavement is slippery
and the hands of sextants smell of tripe
as the locks are afraid of staying locked
every day
and chiefly Easter day
because that day is an old mummy
who has a tooth-ache and munches mica
But the stations covered with sugar
spit on the military
decorated with the CROIX DE GUERRE
the rain will drive all that away
and the sun will dry it again
but on the doorstep of the cottage will remain
a stable-rack half eaten
by the landlord's horse

MAKING FEET AND HANDS

Eye standing up eye lying down eye sitting

Why wander about between two hedges of stair-rails
while the ladders become soft
as new-born babes
as zouaves who lose their homeland with their shoes
Why raise one's arms towards the sky
since the sky has drowned itself
without rhyme or reason
to pass the time and make its moustaches grow
Why does my eye sit down before going to bed
because saddles are making the donkeys sore
and pencils break in the most unpredictable fashion
the whole time
except on stormy days

/ Benjamin Péret

when they break into zigzags
and snowy days
when they tear their sweaters to pieces
But the spectacles the old tarnished spectacles
sing songs while gathering grass for cats
The cats follow the procession
carrying flags
flags and ensigns
The fish's tail crossing a beating heart
the throat regularly rising and falling to imitate the sea surrounding it
and the fish revolving about a ventilator
There are also hands
long white hands with nails of fresh greenery
and finger-joints of dew
swaying eyelashes looking at butterflies
saddened because the day made a mistake on the stairs
There are also sexes fresh as running water
which leap up and down in the valley
because they are touched by the sun
They have no beards but they have clear eyes
and they chase dragonflies
without caring what people will say

THE GIRLS' SCHOOLS ARE TOO SMALL

To Yves Tanguy

The beetles dying of the plague
don't care what railways are like
even though the warmed-up wine
does not prevent the little fish from sleeping
in the light of a lantern
Backwards and forwards
the bread-crumbs pass backwards and forwards
and go into ecstasies at the dogs pissing on the centennial trees
How daring
but daring hat in hand
says shit to you
for you are dull and mouldy
tricoloured and stinking

decorated
decomposed
bearded
worm-eaten
and altogether similar in every respect to an army of fleas on a dirty
carpet

HALF-FIG HALF-GRAPE

If your sweater has a toothache give it an eye-salve
if it has earache
a little mustard
but if grass grows thick and fast
in your gas-pipes
do not hesitate to call in a few
wild and ataxic
hunchbacks
with noses shaped like women's drawers
with a weakness for playing with the ladies under the molehills
A bootbrush in an oven
or a wild strawberry going down the rue des Martyrs on a bicycle
is enough to make the oysters learn to read
and the beans to write
Alas that will never be
for it's raining black-puddings which go ugh when they fall on the
heads of negroes
that will never be for the oranges are bursting like frogs
for the frogs are laughing like dustmen
for the dustmen are singing like tulips
for the tulips are sighing like blue gloves left on a billiard-table
for the billiard-tables are getting bored like locomotives
for

/ Benjamin Péret

LOUIS XVI GOES TO THE GUILLOTINE

Stink stink stink
What stinks
It's Louis XVI the addled egg
and his head falls into the basket
his rotten head
because it's cold on the 21st of January
It's raining blood and snow
and all kinds of filth
spouting out of his ancient corpse
like a dog which has passed out at the bottom of a copper
among the dirty clothes
and has had time to decay
like the pig-bucket fleur-de-lys
which the cows refuse to eat
because it gives off a smell of god
god the father of all dirt
who has given to Louis XVI
the divine right to pass out
like a dog in a copper

STICK NO BILLS

Nevermore shall the wind's bones terrify the old clocks
    howling in the sardine-tins
Nevermore shall the feet of tables put their legs round their necks to
    imitate flies
Nevermore shall broken teeth make music
Nevermore shall loaves of bread walk about naked
Nevermore shall air-currents give orders to statues of salt
Nevermore shall the cross-bar be a railway-signal
Nevermore shall my shaved-off moustache grow again
    above my neighbour's eye
Nevermore shall the beefsteak whistle for its dog
Nevermore shall the metro ask for a drink for pity's sake
Nevermore shall cherry-stones steal latrines
for the least speck of dust the flea which looks for the ears left behind
    in taxis

the hard-boiled eggs which are so good at spying through keyholes
and all that's left of the great wall of China
are there to observe the traditions
and see that the first strawberries are respected
which look at themselves in every mirror
and would be so pleased to see a calf hanging from the butcher's stall
throw itself on to the butcher
and run away after its skin which would be so worn out
that it would see its brother through it.

THE FALL OF THE FRANC

Franc little franc what have you done with your bones
What can they have become but the poker dice
which throws these words on to the paper
as a pansy vicar you used to minister in the corridors of brothels
distributing the host to starved whores
in whose eyes your double image was reflected

And before that your bloated chaps
insulted the skeleton goats
who gave off an old French and Christian smell
as they followed you round like the shadow of a sun

Sun more like a lamp
for you never lit up any but barricaded streets
where the paving-stones were replaced by broken bottles

But today like a worm cut up by dozens of shovels
you are vainly attempting to escape back among the fish
how would you like to become a jesuit leader once again
but the jesuits have died off like rats
and their guts oozing with soft francs
and their eucharistic decay fills all their chalices
as the last survivors appeal to god
Alas god poor worn out franc
lies among the excrements of his priests
Here lies the franc a beet without sugar

/ Benjamin Péret

THE STABILIZATION OF THE FRANC

If the ears of the cows are shivering
it's because the Marseillaise is being sung
Come children of the cow-tub
blow your noses on Poincaré's ear

In vain the macaroni stranded on his beard
murmur
I'm the new franc
Down with the old man who made me boil
Like a cardboard box at a fair
with his eye in the po
Poincaré repeats himself
I well deserved the cow-tub
Long live the congregation of asses
Long live the national cowshed

LITTLE SONG OF THE DISABLED

Lend me your arm
to replace my leg
The rats ate it for me
at Verdun
at Verdun
I ate lots of rats
but they didn't give me back my leg
and that's why I was given the CROIX DE GUERRE
and a wooden leg
and a wooden leg

Francis Ponge (1899 – 1988)

IN SPRING

No smoke without fire?
— In spring, a mouth beneath the earth sucks at cigars that smoulder
with a glow as green as light is in the clearings of the woods.
   A body suffering all the pangs of electrocution since its trans-
formation began, smokes.
   Right under one's nose, the burnt gunpowder smell.
   The scarf tied tightly round the neck behind the cannon–mouth
   After the roar that no one heard
   Unstiffens and floats free.

Gisèle Prassinos (b. 1920)

THESE MESSES ARE MAGNIFICENT

These messes are magnificent
replied my shoe
a smell of elastic
burst its basket
when Prosper alleged his door
by a system of the quarter
a mosquito's antenna
set free the shoemaker
it is true that conical glasses
are cleaner to pick up
for the Pacific Ocean
covered itself with paper
but as I see that Veronica
is making a sauce for the rope-maker
my heart more soft than brick
is going to begin to cry

Raymond Queneau (1903 – 76)

1
Deaf is the night, the shadow, the mist,
Deaf is the tree, deaf the pebble
Deaf is the hammer on the anvil
Deaf is the sea and deaf the owl

Blind the night and blind the stone,
Blind the grass and the ears of corn,
Blind is the mole beneath the ground
Blind a kernel in its fruit.

Dumb is the night and the distress
Dumb are the fields and the prairie,
Dumb is the clearness of the air
Dumb the wood, the lake, the cry.

Sick is the whole of nature,
Sick are the animals and the rocks
Sick is the caricature
Sick the madman who raises the blockade.

But who sees? who hears? who speaks?

2
Death has listened to the inconsistent sermon
Morality's sermon has gone with the wind
Morality's sermon listened to by death
It's death that listens and death that hears
The other talks incessantly and its voice remains
Only as long as a breath gone with the wind
Which listens and hears dumbly and sniffing
The smell of that good sermon above my time
It's my sermon and my death and my time
My nasty smell the dying man's smell
For each day I die and I pray inconsistent
The death of my morality gone with every wind.

1940

Pierre Reverdy *(1889 – 1960)*

REFLUX

When the dazzling smile of the façades rends the morning's fragile décor, when the horizon is still full of lingering sleep, dreams murmuring in the streams under the hedgerows, when the night gathers up its rags which are hanging from low branches, I go out, I make ready, I am more pale and trembling than that page on which not a single line of fate has yet been inscribed. The whole of the distance between you and me – between the life trembling on the surface of my hand and the mortal smile of love nearing its end – wavers and is torn apart. Distance traversed in a single unarrested course, through days without clearness and nights without sleep. And this evening, by making a superhuman effort, I want to shake off all the thickness of this rust – this hungry rust disfiguring my heart and eating my hands away. Why stay for so long buried beneath the debris of the days and of the night, the dust of shadows. And why so much love, so much hatred. A thin blood is boiling with great waves in precious vessels. It runs through the rivers of the body, giving to health all the illusions of victory. But the exhausted traveller, dazzled, hypnotized by the lighthouse's fascinating gleams, is sleeping as he stands, he can no longer resist the magnetic passes of death's hands. This evening I want to spend all the gold of my memory, lay down my too heavy luggage. Nothing is left before my eyes but the naked sky, the walls of the prison which constricted my head, the pavements of the street. One must climb up out of the lower depths of the mine, out of the earth made thick with the humus of sorrow, and once more draw the air into the chest's obscurest crannies, push upwards to the heights – there where the ice is sparkling with all the fire-crackers of conflagration – where the snow is streaming down, the character is hard, among the pitiless tempests of egotism and the peremptory decisions of the mind.

HEARTBREAK

Oh everything's coming to an end
   A slow music's being splashed all over the wall
One hand over the mouth
The other not touching its back
Love escapes through the window naked
The pretty portrait
A woman in a torn chemise weeping
This lofty passion has occasioned grimaces enough
She weeps and departs for heaven which is calling to her
The water and the hardy trees
Despair of love without string music
And yet the trap still remains there hidden
At the cross-roads the barrel-organ one summer evening
Gave your melancholy a sort of meaning
A slight sense of sadness
Nothing's left of it now
All one's friends are dead
The woman went off to meet them of their own accord
You entered the game under an unlucky star
Now what will you be an honest man or a bandit
Nothing
I keep my skin safe under my waistcoat
The following wave rolls on
I launch my smile to float on it
And stare at your reason across the rooftops
The world is gay and everyone laughs and so do you
In a single night I've entirely lost both my age and name.

PERSPECTIVE

Has the same carriage
   Carried me off
          I see where you come from
          You turn your head
Midnight
On the moon

         / Pierre Reverdy

Has ceased striking

               At the street corner
               All has been turned about

I've seen his face
And even his hands

               The last star
               Is in the garden

Like the first one
Tomorrow's coming

               But where will they be
               Dead unawares

When the wall vanishes

               The sky will come down

PORTRAIT

The bed of sombre artificial flowers that grew there has not been
    gathered on the furthest outskirts
The hand drew in a catch of tiny fish that had scarcely been hatched
                    The hand
                    gently
But caught nothing to replace the emptiness
    Neither animals nor people
    Nor lights
  Colour blossoms
                  Fires
         The hand pulled lines back
             through the water
              The air
      Lines living in the midst of night
        The worst thing of all
It also pulled in a noted man's portrait floating
   between two sheets of water showing his beard
But the hand no longer dared return to the border
    Too near the arm and the lace edges
         Talent is nothing

FIGHTING A WAY OUT

Chance when the poet gets near it
When he puts his mouth close to its metal
When he re-reads
Its tentacles and onomatopoeia
He skims the froth off stews
On the rocky foreland
The whirlpools
Lastly the idea of iron
Which hadn't occurred to him
That could only be the other one repenting
The sun rolls over the horizon
The days drag on more slowly
The string and the balloon
The head
The furrow
The instruments gleaming outside the tool-shop
The man approaching
The water going to sleep
And from the mountain here
The feeblest record
Man far from the land
Man in his wonderful dreams

A CONSIDERABLE WAY

Before the boat that does not budge
    Stands one who waits
  It is the port that's moved
    There's too much wind
the tide-level has changed
  how slow soever be the sea
       All grows to greater size
  The passing sailor arrived too late
  What gives him that air of his
      And his head sunk
      By the bar's exit

/ *Pierre Reverdy*

The whole ship's in the rigging
A bird's rubbed out of sight
On the flatter sky
Everyone's scared
When the seamen's cap, and the air and the numbersome faces and
all are whirled by the wind into a single cloud

Georges Ribemont-Dessaignes (1884 – 1974)

SLIDING TROMBONE

I have a little windmill on my head
Which draws up water to my mouth and eyes
When I am hungry or moved to tears
I have a little horn full of the odour of absinth in my ears
And on my nose a green parakeet that flaps its wings
And cries 'Aux Armes'
When from the sky fall the seeds of the sun
The absence from the heart of steel
At the bottom of the boneless and stagnant realities
Is partial to crazy sea–fish
I am the captain and the alsation at the cinema
I have in my belly a little agricultural machine
That reaps and binds electric flex
The cocoanuts thrown by the melancholy monkey
Fall like spittle into the water
Where they blossom again as petunias
I have in my stomach an ocarina and I have virginal faith
I feed my poet on the feet of a pianist
Whose teeth are even and uneven
And sad Sunday evenings
I throw my morganatic dreams
To the loving turtle–doves who laugh like hell.

OPIUM

A queen containing kings in her
A meatball containing queens
The sound of the eyes preventing sleep
And the sleep that prevents one going to sleep
The mouth inside
The blood outside where swim the fiddle-trees
The mouth inside
And death in the middle.

Arthur Rimbaud (1854 – 91)

FROM *THE DESERTS OF LOVE*

FOREWORD

These writings are by a young, a very young *man*, the scene of whose life is of no importance to us. He had no mother, no native land, cared nothing for knowledge and fled from all laws of morality, as many pitiable young men had already fled before him. But he, so divided by boredom and torment – where did this lead him but towards death, as towards a fatal, terrible indecency. Not having loved women – though his blood ran high! – he had brought up his soul and his heart in ways strangely mistaken and sad. From the following dreams, – his loves! – which came to him in his bed or in the street, a few gentle religious considerations may perhaps be drawn. One will call to mind the continual sleep of the legendary Mohammedans, who were, however, both honest and circumcised! But, this bizarre suffering being possessed of a disturbing authority, it is sincerely to be desired that this Soul, led astray among us all, and who wishes for death, it seems, should meet in that instant with true consolations, and be worthy of them.

I

This time, it is the Woman I saw in the Town, and to whom I have spoken, and who speaks to me.

I was in a room where there was no light. Someone came to tell me that she was in my house: and I saw her in my bed, all mine, and without light! I was very moved, and largely because it was my family's house: I was also seized by distress! I was in rags, and she, worldly-wise and offering herself: she had to go away! A nameless distress: I took her, and let her fall out of the bed, almost naked; and, in my unutterable weakness, I fell upon her and dragged myself with her upon the carpets, without light! The family lamp was filling the neighbouring rooms with a ruddy glow one after the other. Then the woman disappeared. I shed more tears than God has ever been able to demand.

I went out into the endless town. O weariness! Drowned in the heavy night and in the flight of happiness. It was like a night in winter, with a snowfall to stifle the world once and for all. The friends to whom I cried out to ask where she was staying gave me false replies. I stood before the windows of the place where she goes every evening: I ran into a garden wrapped in sleep. I was pushed out. I wept copiously at all this. At last, I went down into a place that was full of dust and, sitting down on some timbers, I wept all night until there were no tears left in my body. – And yet my exhaustion kept coming back to me.

I realized she had gone back to her everyday life; and that the happy moment would take longer to return than the cycle of a star. She did not come back, and never will come back, the Adorable one who came to give herself to me, – which I should never have presumed. Truly, this time I have wept more than all the children in the world.

II

It is certainly the same countryside. The same rustic house of my parents; the same room with arms and lions above the door. At dinner there is a long room with candles and wines and antique wainscotting. The dinner table is very large. The servants! there were many of them, as far as I remember. – One of my old friends was there, a priest and dressed as a priest: in order to be more free. I remember his room hung with purple, with windows of yellow paper; and his books, hidden away, which had been dipped in the ocean!

I was left alone in this endless country house: reading in the kitchen, drying the bottoms of my clothes in front of the guests, while conversations went on in the drawing-room; excessively moved by the murmur of the morning milk and of the night of the last century.

I was in a very dark room: what was I doing there? A servant came near me: I may say that it was a little dog; though how beautiful she was and, to me, of an indescribable maternal nobility: pure, unstrange and wholly charming! She pinched my arm.

I can no longer even recall her face clearly: it does not recall to me her arm, the skin of which I rolled between two fingers; nor her mouth, which my own mouth seized like a little despairing wave, endlessly wearing something away. I upset her into a basket of cushions and ships' canvas, in a dark corner. I can recall nothing more than her white lace knickers.

Then, O despair! the partition turned vaguely into the shadows of the trees, and I was overwhelmed by the amorous sadness of the night.

1871

/ Arthur Rimbaud

Gui Rosey (b. 1896)

ANDRÉ BRETON

Burning the seas
the brain of the seas
the illustrious maniac crowned with snowy musics
compared the future to his clever ring
compared without knowing it the mediaeval birds and the storms'
    sceptre
eternally compared eternity and tears
like the submarine lamps in which the renewal of dead things is
    woven
but you arrive more nobly than a glacier
and hold out to me a hand that the cold changes into a lotus flower
which renders you dramatically invisible and tender
under the thousand and one vulnerable nights in the place that is
    most dear to us
the same woman shared between two evils like the wrong sides of
    our hearts
the same broken line of heteroclite fatigues
and our fear of living alone with our eyes

Others will say what your voice was among the painted lips like
    moving castles
I do not guide the death that comes decked with celestial frivolities
with footsteps accessory to timid odours
along the ghostly stairways breaking the spell of tamed countries
where you breathe the air of amber exchanges and almond griefs
many elements of sadness here unveil their theatrical cuts
giving passage to thousands of untold treasures that no longer know
    how to run
skeletons of shadow beneath the wigs of days commemorated by
    the cascading tares
of imponderable vernal writings
simulating the generosity of springs
on the medal of a century on which
your gesture poses like a solar ghost for history

Hardly will my effort end in beauty
with carnal graces above the indignity of tombs
at the tormented base of inexhaustible hooped laughter
false manners of pearl releasing the clutch of a chrysalis
at the zenith of this barbarous reign of thought
which is worth everything in its place
like a phantom behind each word

How many obsolete mothers must there be
and how many punctual devourers of treasures
before a privilege rises to the lips
at the height of days that have attained the hallucinatory perfection
    of cold
forever in a new state like madness
latent like a sigh parallel to the horizon weakly sustained
by the sculptural applause of excessive truths.

/ Gui Rosey

Philippe Soupault (1897 – 1990)

THE HERMIT-CRAB SAYS:

FEELINGS ARE FREE

Trace smell of sulphur
Marsh of public health-measures
Red of criminal lips
March two-time pickle-brine
Monkeys' caprice
Day-coloured clock

OVATION

Heat of Sunday-stopped railway-engines
Prostitutes' dust-coat
Marine problem moon
Solid meridians hive
Calomel of childhoods at the theatre
Blue countrysides
There are three inhabitants
Flying-fish in love with the stars
The rivers beard langour
Occident
Millenium compass
Psychologist pharmacists are a public danger
Fury of Chicago factories
Rite
Men love the pallor of animals

REGULATIONS

Reddened pins
Anxious sleep of the fathers of families
Table of sugared values
The angling of arguments is for sale

Paper flight bloody handkerchief
Academic occupations the ewe is rambling in the five-star hotels
Marriage-bed of mirrors
Republican stars
My tongue animal of rich bourgeois layabouts
Sighs of happy mothers

THE PERMANENT MODES

Crime of adolescents Epsom salts
River of chapped hands
Palace of festivals and dawns
Red red the song
Blanched sensations
Courage virgin blotter
A fly makes old men scared
A brain is discovered there are red ants
March
March
Alleluia

BULLETINS

The colourless gases are in abeyance
Two thousand three hundred scruples
Snow of the well-springs
Smiles are acknowledged
Don't give sailors' promises
The lions of the poles
The sea the sea the natural sand
The grey parrot of poor parents
Country sojourn of the oceans
7 o'clock in the evening
Night of the land of rabies
Finances sea-salt
Summer's lovely hand is alone to be seen
The cigarettes of the dying

/ *Philippe Soupault*

THE MANUFACTORIES

The foreign animals and the generals of industry are in the same circle
The avenue of kisses
Young people's illness
The paper of the wall, of beds, of cages and circuses
Salutations' studios
A dance quick a dance
Delicate chemistry
Throw the dice
A man at sea
A man is passing I want to see him
He is running blue bluer than my frozen fingers the rails' stain
The railway the factories
The iron is burning
The wood
The tobacco of prisons mother of dreams
A bar crossroad–circus unhealthy gallantry
Thursday thursday
Take your hand the head of the trees
Calm of the suns
Compound substances salt
Lorries, bring us the results
The shades our girl–friends
A general gives hands an order
The beautiful watches

ETERNITY

Opening of griefs one two one two
They're toads the red flags
The saliva of flowers
Electrolysis the glorious dawn
Child's balloon of the suburb's smoke
The clods of earth cornetfull of sand
Dear tolerated child you are panting
Never prosecuted the mauve light of knocking shops
The carpet is bordered with nests of dead leaves
House–movings followed by village choral societies
On the walls for fete–days are affixed eyes the playthings of the poor

Farewell source of diseases
All the cries every one and those that remain are liquid
For grown-ups the red order
House sun dance forgetting the veils of fog
Summer, moon
The lantern and the little grey tree that bears an exotic name
0 133 those are the fingers of ataxics the field's vines
Biology teaches love
Weave lucid truths
My head has been wrapped up in a bandage
Crime or suicide
Acetylene is a white carnation
The frightful eyeglasses

COMMANDMENTS

Lottery of ascents and of China asters
People play for the thousand tears of sensitive youth at cards
Title of the dearly beloveds
The honey of brows passes to distances calculated on the working
    night
The differing ills of streets gay days of sweetened Saturdays
Metal mouth setting sun
Compressed air is a disgrace
Who wants to sing the ballad of burns

        Pretty is a rose
        A fan of reflexes
        Milk's colour reposes
        On this wild west of riches

        The most gracious contraptions
        And the hateful clothes-dealers
        Offer our wheedling conceptions
        The smokes of gratitude

There is so much to be read in these passages
Our veins are bursting rockets
Humidity corrodes our feelings of selected shades

Our yellow Sunday leisures
Register of numbered passions
Matches are excellent and blossom at every turn
Long live the cerebellum of mice

ON THE TOWERS' THRESHOLD

The waves of miracles and deeds
The divine reckoning of palaces
Thanks for all these members
A solid carpet a sword-stick and the glory of exiles
The numbers of horizons scarlet tongue inclinations
Why bow the noble or struggling head
Days pass across the hands
Little flame for persons blind from birth
Demonstration of laughs brown school at the end of the village blue
    smoke of charcoal-burners and alpine rangers
A rainbow sorcerer shepherd
The light comes like a fount
Physics don't count any more
These long wires and telegrams are the flowers of our rose-coloured
    civilisations
One must care for one's neighbours for the smells of the nights and
    morrows
The college, window decked with ivy
The gallop of camels
Lost port
The station's on the right station café *Bifur* That's fear
Oceanic prefectures
I hide myself in a historic picture
So green that it's going to blossom
The leaves are loving sighs
Hastily cut your desires three escaped mast-poles mad dancers
The sea has no more colour come and see the sea of algae
The gilliflower map of the world or shark
The poor giraffe's on the right
The seal is wailing
The inspectors have darknesses and kingfishers in their hands a
    graphometer animal of dry cities
For you lost stamens General staff of cold eternities

The bottles of flame are sweet so sweet
The suburban pirates have blacked eyes
Brightness green adoration of landscapes
Polished shoes
Industrial company without title-deed The chemical association of
    clocks
Looseness of eyeless rodents
Morbid hungers of the pale broody hens
Mauve naïvety of the dealers in rapid and brutally scooped-out
    shutters
Under the eye of adopted acids the lighthouses inspire courage
Green water for women
Day-before-yesterday's papers grannies talk rubbish the sky is blue
    the sea is blue eyes are blue
Musical rays quadrupeds indolent broadswords
The wasps torn to pieces are mute they are tearful tunnel-trap spiders
    The sack of submarine cities pigeons are present the chandeliers
    cut the walls and brains
There are always alarm-clocks
The basilica of startled seconds
The importance of barometers flat fish
Basil and mignonette
Spanish dances the cliff of gestures scaffolding of torrents
A sphere destroys all

From *Les Champs Magnétiques* (1920)

147   / *Philippe Soupault*

Jules Supervielle (1884 – 1960)

POEM

I'm all alone above the sea
With feet mounting on ladder-rungs
That stretch straight up out of the waves.
I have to touch my face at times
To make sure that it's really mine
And that I'm here, so strange it seems.
More ladder-rungs ever-renewed
And I'm a little nearer heaven,
What little's possible to men.
Oh! I've begun to feel weighed down
With such a heavy weariness,
For I don't rise ever-renewed
As does the ladder I am on.
Shall I let go with these two hands
That are of use to me now less
To hold on with than understand?
I've slipped I'll be one with the waves!
First wet then water I become,
Now splash-foamed and now smooth again.
The poet's gone down in the deep
And left no flotsam trace behind.

RAIN AND THE TYRANTS

I stand and watch the rain
Falling in pools which make
Our grave old planet shine;
The clear rain falling, just the same
As that which fell in Homer's time
And that which dropped in Villon's day
Falling on mother and child
As on the passive backs of sheep;

Rain saying all it has to say
Again and yet again, and yet
Without the power to make less hard
The wooden heads of tyrants or
To soften their stone hearts,
And powerless to make them feel
Amazement as they ought;
A drizzling rain which falls
Across all Europe's map,
Wrapping all men alive
In the same moist envelope;
Despite the soldiers loading arms,
Despite the newspapers' alarms,
Despite all this, all that,
A shower of drizzling rain
Making flags hang wet.

STRANGERS' FACES

Faces that turn to shine of sun
To tumbling rain, to hostile fate,
Summer and Winter faces both,
Absorbed in dream or common day,
You in your night of limbs and hearts
Are like storm-lanterns' trusty wicks
and even though fever-lit your eyes
Burn like such trimmed lamps' faithful lights.
Thanks to those staunchly shining specks
Emitting gleams between your lids
You find your way beneath the stars
Bare faces topping trunks full-dressed.
Yours were children's faces once
But then without moving a step
They went on till they looked grown-up

Men and women in the street
Who cross and pass without a word,
A populace of statues with

No plinths but ever ambling round
With dangling arms and arid eyes,
Doesn't it seem like rubbing sleeves
With nothingness, to have to keep
Silent your troubles, care-worn ones?
O faces full of still-born words
Still searching outlet into speech
O persecuted visages
You hunt yourselves down but can't see
Each other, find yourselves alone
And on a sudden lost at last
You yield to lips elusive still
As each to other drawing nigh
Buries his face on his brother's neck.

ALTER EGO

Hark! a mouse scuffling by!
(That wasn't a mouse)
It's scared one of the maids
(How do you know it has?)
And now the door creaks
(Why, its hinge just oiled!)
In the garden-close wall
(That wall's been pulled down)
Oh, there's naught I can say!
(Then why not hold your tongue?)
I must stay still stuck fast
(You're out for a walk)
Where *does* this road go?
(That's what I'd like to know)
I'm alone on this earth
(I am close by your side)
Can one be so alone?
(I'm more lonely than you.
Your face I can see.
No one ever saw mine).

WHILE THERE'S LIFE

Still plenty of night-blue
Sky above trees,
Still plenty of fruit
On stone table to heap,
As much dark as it needs
To make blood beat beat,
And enough purity
To preserve the heart's red,
A sufficiently bright
Ray of light on white page,
And enough love to fill
Up all silence's depths
While the sorry soul still
Its thirst begs to slake,
The thread that runs through
All our days each day thins,
And the heart's slowly dulled
By the hard-pressing years,
But for us none would know
From the creak of the well
The turned handle was drawing
Up one more full pail.

FROM *NOCTURNE IN BROAD DAY*

Trees, in spite of the trend of events,
And cedar, more cedar than ever in spite of the war,
You with your head outspreading up beyond the cares of men,
And grass, as thick in growth as your indifference is great,
Not to mention birds and insects, all as far away
In our cupped hands as in the sky's inhuman depths,
Not to mention the earth quite inattentive at our feet,
Sure of finding itself again when all catastrophes are past,
The Earth whose earth flung into air falls back to fill all holes,
And let us not speak of our organs which understand nothing that
     takes place,

Receiving undecipherable signals from our nerves
And leaving the brain to shake off its anxiety alone
Like a drenched dog shaking off the water from its coat.
But the brain lives hidden and retired within itself,
Alone exposed to every blow inside the small box of the skull
And doomed to manufacture silence night and day
Out of even the most wild and argumentative ideas
Such as are never heard outside where men pass to and fro.

(La Fable du Monde)

FIVE THOUSAND METRES DOWN

To R. Güiraldes

When the gooseberry bush which grows on the sea-bed
Keeps watch far from all eyes over its berries growing ripe;
Comparing one fruit with another in its heart,
And when the eucalyptus-tree of the abyss,
Five thousand liquid metres down, is brooding hopelessly on some
    lost scent,
Then down towards the ocean harvests phosphorescent workers glide,
While others with wet shining palms go searching after happiness
Or for the colour of their children who are still opaque as yet
And grow-up undiscovered by themselves
Among the seaweeds and the pearls.
Through tumbling, salty liquid masses love goes plunging on
While joy is as evasive as a melancholy mood.
As though in church one makes one's way beneath cascades of gloom
Which make no foam, no sound.
Sometimes one guesses up above a cloud is drifting over the free sky,
Directed doubtless in its course by some wise-miened coast-dwelling
    child.
Then one by one the deeps' lighthouses show their beams
Which are more violently pitch-black than blackness;
Which revolve.

(Gravitations)

MARSEILLES

Marseilles that emerged from the sea, with its rock-fish, its shells
    and its iodine,
And its masts in the midst of the town which contend for the passers-
    by,
Its trams with their crustacean claws are shining with sea-water,
The splendid rendez-vous of live men who raise their arms as though
    claiming their share of the sky,
And the pavements spawn on the pavements men and women of
    today with their eyes of phosphorus,
Their glasses, their cups, their ice-buckets and their drinks,
And all that makes a noise of feet and of jumping chairs.
Here the sun thinks aloud, it's a great light that joins in the
    conversation,
And rejoices the throats of women as the torrents do those in the
    mountain*,
It takes the new-comers aside, jostles them a little in the street,
And without a word pushes them over onto the side of the pretty
    girls.
And the moon is a monkey escaped from a sailor's knapsack
That watches you through the slight bars of the night.
Marseilles, listen to me, I beg of you, pay attention,
I'd like to take you into a corner, talk to you quietly,
So stay a little so we can look at each other a little,
O city forever departing
And that can never go away
Because of all those anchors nibbling away at you under the sea.

From *Débarcadères*

---

* (*Translator's note*: Untranslatable pun in this line: *gorge*, both throat and mountain-
    gorge)

HOMAGE TO LIFE

It's fine to have chosen
Domicile for life
And to lodge the time
In a continual heart,
And to have seen one's hands
Setting themselves on the world
As they would on an apple
In a little garden,
To have loved the earth
The moon and the sun
Like familiar friends
Who are irreplaceable,
And to have entrusted
The world to one's memory
Like a light horseman
To his black mount,
To have given a face
To these words: wife, children,
And served as a shore
To wandering continents,
And to have reached the soul
With little oar-strokes
So as not to scare it
By a brusque approach,
It's fine to have known
The shade beneath the foliage
And to have felt age
Crawl on the naked body,
Accompanied the pain
Of the black blood in the veins
And made golden one's silence
With the star of Patience,
And to have all these words
Stirring in one's head
To choose the least lovely
To fête them a little,
To have felt life
Hasty and ill-loved
To have enclosed it
In this poetry.

Jean Tardieu (1903 – 95)

TOMBEAU DE HÖLDERLIN

The day the day hums with confused rebukes
The night complains and complains
it complains without saying why

The rising sun
speaks to us like a father
but we don't listen to its advice

Space is inhabited by numberless fires
which send us signals we can never understand
and time for a long while
worries our memory
like a face it's impossible to find again.
Alone after a long day's walk
often I go to the foot of that shadow-show
and before the empty stage
I watch with anguished heart
calling without echo
to those great actors who for a hundred thousand years
have reigned over our ingratitude
and speak without being heard.

Forest, why keep silence still?
Awaken and step out! O sky,
why close your eyes in broad daylight?
Mingle with the sun's gold chains
the hidden treasures of your Night! Let times
be mixed, and everything,
past present future, be together given
to the indomitable spirit which is hoping for you
and awaits you!...
                    And if, from this tumult,
a unique voice emerges, that with its quietness
can dominate the thunder, and that Smile
stronger than the mortal combat of the elements,
then may we learn at last

from the unalterable peace
the seed of which lies in the spirit of men
since the first day!

But none finds in himself other reply
than his own heart's sound, and ever the silence
alone seems to announce the word, and evermore
in us the immense voices fade away
with the remembrance of the Promise
like a withdrawing storm.

Une Voix sans personne (1954)

Georg Trakl *(1887 – 1914)*

THE SUN

(Adapted)

Every day the yellow sun comes on to the hill,
Fair, the forest, the swart beast,
The man; huntsman or shepherd.

The fish rises ruddy in the green pond.
Under the full round sky
The fisherman steers the blue boat.

Slowly ripens the grape cluster, the corn.
When peaceably the day declines,
Good and evil are at hand.

When the night falls
The traveller slowly lifts heavy lids.
From a gloomy gully surges a glint of sun.

(December 1913)

With acknowledgement to Marc Petit and Jean-Claude Schneider

Tristan Tzara (1896 – 1963)

[UNTITLED]

in your inside there are smoking lamps
the swamp of blue honey
cat crouched in the gold of a flemish inn
boom boom
lots of sand yellow bicyclist
chateauneuf des papes
manhattan there are tubs of excrement before you
mbaze mbaze bazebaze melaganga garoo
you turn rapidly inside me
kangaroos in the boat's entrails

THE APPROXIMATE MAN

(Fragment)

the mountains' whooping-cough charring the escarpments of the
     gorges
in the pestiferous buzzings of autumnal aqueducts
cultivation of the gratuitous sky, communal ditch snapped at by so
     many crystalline pastures
the languages of nudes brief apparitions of messengers
in their annunciatory tufts of supreme clamours and obsessions
the restless underground chemical-works lagging like songs
the swiftness of rain its raw telegraphic tingling of ruminating shell
pick-axes' crude punctures whence frothing lye emerges
broken on all the landscapes and on the tricks of the jeering valleys
     tempting the nations
the godless promenades of water-courses
the temerity of their exploits against the seated dusk of clay
the forgetting of captive essences drowned in the forgetting of numbers
     and ferries
and the fibrous dungeons heaped with corn-ears and bells
where spinners of cares disappear in the darkness quaking with
     scythes

and open visual capsules at the end of the sexual icicles of ghosts
the rawness of the kernels of stone walls climbed by a thousand
    fingers
interlacing themselves with dandelion tresses
and the pathetic balancing of temperatures raked by the excessive
    gaze

your complacences set up in me too sweet a meandering of easy and
    sleeping oracle
and flinty in my clothes of slate I have devoted my watching
to the torment of the oxydised desert
and to the robust accession of fire

crushed against the basaltic dumbness of the ibises
hanging from the bridles of underground rivers
a prey to mad forests of hydras
where the thick summers' sermons gargle dreamy rivalries
night swallows us up and casts us out to the other end of the lair
moving beings whom the eyes' grammar has not yet defined upon
    the area of to-morrow
slow coral encirclings
disgorge the high forks of rocky wills
the cantles of your heart a heavy weather of gravel
and how many barracks in the shelter of your forehead have written
    the wide mourning of moss on the breast
falling in ruin of masses of futures
covered with embroiled loads mixed with the lianas' clumsy
    ambushes
where the ridges of troubles and fishes let opaque death and tresses
    trickle through them

we were going on to moors made sweet by attention
sweetly attentive to the monotonous jolts of the phenomena
that the ungrateful exercise of the infinite printed on the blocks of
    perception
but the scaly structure of scarce opinions
on the damp infinity of diadems – the fields –
disdains truths' palpable pulp
with a ready favour of quickened punishment
axes were hacking among roan laughter
and the disks of the hours flew to the attack
burst in the head of the aerial herds

/ Tristan Tzara

it was our reasons lying fallow that were stemming their diaphanous
    turbulence
and the knotty trajects that they traced in time
had a tentacular incarnation in the constraint of clay

there we abandoned the pleasure and the dogma of the spectacle
and sacrificed to other impulses the goldenbrown desire that its fruit
    brought to us
mow down, diamantine insistances, the vain landscapes elaborated
    by my senses
deaf upright hallucinating distrust
on the turntable of my being all the roads are open to you
carry away what the drunkenness of reproach has not yet known
    how to throw down
and everything that I could once understand and in which I believe
    no more
and the clot of those things that I could not understand which rises
    to my throat
and the seawrack tanned by the implacable toil of the depths
and the flower of the triangle incised on the pupil
and the battle lost by my breath on the stiff white page
and the osmosis of odious thoughts
and the sorrows riddled by persistent sowings of seduction
and the voluted hut of dust
and that of the lost soul
and so many others and so many others
recovered or ill
for flinty in my clothes of slate I have devoted my watching
to the torment of the oxydised desert
to the robust accession of fire

hands strangely secluded from clusters of transparent hands
mingle with the dominoes of stars upon the savanna they are sheep
and the barks of crushed clouds of nautical odours linger
on the table of the sky encumbered with eucharistic games
what games what savage joys feed with disarray your proceeding
    into the sky of acclimatisation
where wild beasts and planets roll entwined with opium eyes
stretched out from end to end of the aquarium your heart so
    luminously slashed with silence
dedicated to the careful tricks of the blades
incrusted with rebellious drops of wine and with impious words

drinks in the coming and going of ecstasies in the verbal congestion
   whose typhoon stigmatises your forehead

carven henceforth is the prow of the ramparts according to the way
   they swim
but now your eyes guide the cyclone
lofty tenebrous intention
and at sea as far as the limits of the bird vigils
the wind coughs as far as the limit where death discharges
promethean cataracts of echoes thunder into our benumbed
   consciousness
it means suffering when the earth remembers you and shakes you off
beaten and poor village dog you wander
and ceaselessly return the point of departure unconsoled with the
   word
a flower in the corner of your mouth a phthisic flower knocked about
   by the rough necropolis
tons of wind are poured out into the deaf citadel of fever
a skittle at the mercy of a thoughtless movement what am I
an unconsoled point of departure to which I return smoking the
   word in the corner of my mouth
a flower beaten by the rugged fever of the wind
and flinty in my clothes of slate I have devoted my watching
to the torment of the oxydised desert
to the robust accession of fire

when the ramifications of chance fasten on to the ropes by means of
   their smile
when your heart is called – there where the solid bits sink down
dusty and sour moth – dull intimacy – what do I know – shipyard of
   night
when the beaten-up jar full of whistlings of sharp-edged reptiles'
   frill
in which rave the madreporic solicitations of male inclemencies
rumbles at length and moans
a slow furnace of invincible constancy – man –
a slow furnace rises up from the bottom of your slow gravity
a slow furnace rises up from the valley of the chief glaciers
a slow furnace of unspeakable alloys
a slow furnace which reaches the hearths of the lucid emotions
a wide furnace rises up from the enslaved coughings of fortresses
a slow fire quickens to the gaping dread of your strength – man –

a fire quickens the heights of nymph where the coastings of stratus
have earthed-up the taste of gulf
a fire that climbs up the suppliant ladder as far as the stains of the
limitless gestures
a fire that barks out shouts of regret above the hypocritical suggestions
of possibility
a fire that escapes from the muscular seas where plays the unconscious
with speedy flights – man –
a man who shakes with the indefinable presumptions of mazes of
fire
a fire that warps the swelling mass revolt of letters – folds itself up
harmony – may this word be banished from the feverish world I visit
of ferocious affinities dug out of nothingness covered with murders
that yells at not breaking down the sobbing barrier of shreds of
flamingoes
for the fire of anger varies the animation of the subtle wrecks
according to the stuttering modulations of hell
that your heart exhaustedly recognises among the dizzy volleys of
stars
and flinty in my clothes of slate
I have devoted my watching to the oxydised desert of torment
to the robust accession of its flames

(1929)

APPENDIX

Sources of the Poems

GUILLAUME APOLLINAIRE
Francis Picabia. Unpublished MS

ANDRÉ BRETON
The Spectral Attitudes. *A Short Survey of Surrealism* (1935)
Postman Cheval. *Contemporary Poetry and Prose* (June 1936)
Cards on the Dunes. Unpublished typescript
The Hermit-Crab Says. 1st poem-sequence. *The Magnetic Fields* (1985)

ANDRÉ BRETON and PAUL ELUARD
Force of Habit. *A Short Survey of Surrealism* (1935)

BLAISE CENDRARS
Mee Too Buggi. Unpublished MS

RENÉ CHAR
The Raving Messengers of Frantic Poetry. *Contemporary Poetry and Prose* (June 1936)
Georges Braque Intra Muros. *Adam* 419/421 (1979)
Narrow Altar. *Aquarius* 12 (1980)

XIE CHUANG
The Darkening Garden. *Mir Poets* 18 (1988)

RENÉ DAUMAL
The Poet's Last Words. *Atlas Anthology 2* (1984)

YVES DE BAYSER
A Selection of Poems from *Inscrire*. *Temenos* 2 (1980)

ROBERT DESNOS
There was a Leaf. *Argo* (Autumn 1981)

ANDRÉ DU BOUCHET
Cable. Unpublished MS

PAUL ELUARD
One for All. *New Verse* (February 1934)
The Sheep. *A Short Survey of Surrealism* (1935)
'At the End of a Long Voyage'. *A Short Survey of Surrealism* (1935)
What the Workman Says... *A Short Survey of Surrealism* (1935)
Statement. *Contemporary Poetry and Prose* (June 1936)
From *Like an Image*. *Contemporary Poetry and Prose* (June 1936)
All the Rights. *Contemporary Poetry and Prose* (June 1936)
Arp. *Contemporary Poetry and Prose* (June 1936)
Necessity. *Contemporary Poetry and Prose* (June 1936)

163

At Present. *New Verse* (June–July 1936)
Critique of Poetry. *Man's Life Is This Meat* (1936)
A Woman. *Thorns of Thunder* (1936)
Georges Braque. *Thorns of Thunder* (1936)
Giorgio de Chirico. *Thorns of Thunder* (1936)
André Masson. *Thorns of Thunder* (1936)
Beauty and Resemblance. *Thorns of Thunder* (1936)
Poetic Objectivity. *Thorns of Thunder* (1936)
Void. *Thorns of Thunder* (1936)
A Personality Always New. *Thorns of Thunder* (1936)
Humphrey Jennings. *London Bulletin* 11 (March 1939)
'Yesterday's Conquerors Shall Perish'. *Poetry (London)* (March 1942)
Death of a Monster. *New Road* 4 (1946)
Hunted. British Library Add. MS 56042
Sisters of Hope. British Library Add. MS 56045
Max Ernst. Unpublished typescript
Balthus. *Illuminations* (Summer 1993)

PIERRE EMMANUEL
Asia. *The Window* (February 1954)

JEAN FOLLAIN
Some Poems from *Présent Jour*. 1–17: *Poetry Nation Review* 12 (1979)
    18–20: *Stand*, Vol. 21, No. 2 (1980)

BENJAMIN FONDANE
Poem 1933. *Poetry Nation Review* 12 (1979)
Two Poems from *Au Temps du Poème, 1944. Pennine Platform* I (1980)

ANDRÉ FRENAUD
But Who's Afraid? *The Third Eye (Psychic Issue)*. (February–April 1984)

EUGÈNE GUILLEVIC
Memory. *Argo* (Spring 1980)

MAURICE HENRY
The Bronze Piano. *Contemporary Poetry and Prose* (June 1936)

FRIEDRICH HÖLDERLIN
Song of Destiny. *Hölderlin's Madness* (1938)
The Half of Life. *Hölderlin's Madness* (1938)
Ages of Life. *Hölderlin's Madness* (1938)
The Harvest. *Hölderlin's Madness* (1938)
Patmos. *Hölderlin's Madness* (1938)

'And Little Knowledge But Much Pleasure'. *Hölderlin's Madness* (1938)
Native Land. *Hölderlin's Madness* (1938)
Prince of the Air. *Hölderlin's Madness* (1938)
The Eagle. *Hölderlin's Madness* (1938)
Sybil. *Hölderlin's Madness* (1938)
Form and Spirit. *Hölderlin's Madness* (1938)
To the Beloved (Diotima). *Hölderlin's Madness* (1938)
'Am I Not Far From Thee'. *Hölderlin's Madness* (1938)
'Peacefully the Neckar'. *Hölderlin's Madness* (1938)
Greece. *Hölderlin's Madness* (1938)
Autumn. *Hölderlin's Madness* (1938)
Winter. *Hölderlin's Madness* (1938)
Spring. *Hölderlin's Madness* (1938)
Summer. *Hölderlin's Madness* (1938)
Perspectives. *Hölderlin's Madness* (1938)
Tinian. *Collected Verse Translations* (1970)
'O sure foundations of the Alps'. *Collected Verse Translations* (1970)
Remembrance. *Collected Verse Translations* (1970)
Fragment (And in that far off distance...). From MS notebook (1949/50)
The Walk. *For David Gascoyne on his sixty-fifth birthday* (1981)
The Churchyard. Unpublished typescript
To Zimmer. *Poems for Charles Causley* (1982)
Sunday. *Poems for Charles Causley* (1982)

GEORGES HUGNET
Poem (The chrysalis says...). *A Short Survey of Surrealism* (1935)
Poem (A mail-coach overturns...). *A Short Survey of Surrealism* (1935)

EDMOND JABÈS
The Farewell. *Temenos* 13 (1992)

MAX JACOB
They Key. Unpublished typescript
The True Miracles. Unpublished typescript
Glimmers in the Darkness. Unpublished typescript

PIERRE JEAN JOUVE
Woman and Earth. *Poems 1937-1942* (1943)
The Moths. *Poetry (London)* (March–April 1941)
Brow. *Poems 1937-1942* (1943)
Nada. *Poetry (London)* (March–April 1941)
The Two Witnesses. *Poems 1937-1942* (1943)

The Desires of the Flesh... *New Road* 4 (1946)
Transpierce Me Lord... *New Road* 4 (1946)
A Lone Woman Asleep. *New Road* 4 (1946)
From *Nul N'en Etait Témoin*. *New Road* 4 (1946)
Insula Monti Majoris. *Folios of New Writing* (Spring 1940)
Gravida. *New Road* 4 (1946)
When Glory's Spring Returns. *Poetry (London)* (September–October 1947)
From *Sueur de Sang*. *Poetry (London)* September–October 1947)
From *Langue*. *London Magazine* (February 1955)
Freedom or Death. British Library Add. MS 56045
In Helen's Land. *Selected Poems* (1994)
Evening Prayer. *Selected Poems* (1994)
From *Génie*. From notebook 3 (c.1950)
To Himself. From notebook 3 (c.1950)
Pietà (fragment). From notebook 4 (c.1950)
[untitled]. Here the sky... From a 1950 notebook

VALERY LARBAUD
London. Unpublished typescript
Weston-Super-Mare: Noon. *Pennine Platform* 3 (March 1982)

GIACOMO LEOPARDI
An Imitation of Leopardi's Imitation Canto (XXV). *Mir Poets* 18 (1988)
A Se Stesso/To Himself. After Canto XXVIII. Enitharmon Press (1985)

STÉPHANE MALLARMÉ
Summer Sadness. *Babel*, Vol. 1, No. 3 (Summer 1940)

LOYS MASSON
Poem of the Forms of Grace. *Modern Poetry in Translation* (1983)
The Pastor Essendean... *Modern Poetry in Translation* (1983)

O.V. DE L. MILOSZ
H. Enitharmon Poetry Pamphlets 2 (1993)
Unfinished Symphony. Enitharmon Poetry Pamphlets 2 (1993)
Canticle of Spring. Enitharmon Poetry Pamphlets 2 (1993)
The Bridge. Enitharmon Poetry Pamphlets 2 (1993)
Psalm of the Morning Star. *Temenos* 2 (1982)

BENJAMIN PÉRET
That's No Good. *Contemporary Poetry and Prose* (June 1936)
The Staircase with a Hundred Steps. *Contemporary Poetry and Prose* (August–September 1936)

And So On. *A Short Survey of Surrealism* (1935)
Honest Folk. *A Short Survey of Surrealism* (1935)
Slapped Face. *A Bunch of Carrots* (1936)
At the End of the World. *A Bunch of Carrots* (1936)
A Bunch of Carrots. *A Bunch of Carrots* (1936)
Flanders Bridge. *A Bunch of Carrots* (1936)
Making Feet and Hands. *A Bunch of Carrots* (1936)
The Girls' Schools are too Small. *A Bunch of Carrots* (1936)
Half-fig Half-grape. *A Bunch of Carrots* (1936)
Louis XVI Goes to the Guillotine. *A Bunch of Carrots* (1936)
Stick No Bills. *A Bunch of Carrots* (1936)
The Fall of the Franc. *A Bunch of Carrots* (1936)
The Stabilization of the Franc. *A Bunch of Carrots* (1936)
Little Song of the Disabled. *A Bunch of Carrots* (1936)

FRANCIS PONGE
In Spring. Unpublished typescript

GISÈLE PRASSINOS
These Messes are Magnificent. British Library Add. MS 56042

RAYMOND QUENEAU
Deaf is the night... *Pennine Platform* 1 (1980)
Death has listened... *Pennine Platform* 1 (1980)

PIERRE REVERDY
Reflux. *Mandrake* (Winter 1946)
Heartbreak. *The Window* 7 (1954)
Perspective. *The Window* 7 (1954)
Portrait. *The Window* 7 (1954)
Fighting a Way Out. *The Window* 7 (1954)
A Considerable Way. British Library Add. MS 56060

GEORGES RIBEMONT-DESSAIGNES
Sliding Trombone. *New Verse* (December 1933)
Opium. *Argo* (incorporating *Delta*, Autumn 1981)

ARTHUR RIMBAUD
From *The Deserts of Love*. *Contemporary Poetry and Prose* (Spring
    1937)

GUI ROSEY
André Breton. *Contemporary Poetry and Prose* (June 1936)

PHILIPPE SOUPAULT
The Hermit-Crab Says. 2nd poem-sequence. *The Magnetic Fields*
    (1985)

DATE DUE

UPI   PRINTED IN U.S.A.